MANAGERIAL ECONOMICS OF NON-PROFIT ORGANISATIONS

Managerial Economics of Non-Profit Organisations

Marc Jegers

VUBPRESS

Brussels University Press

Cover design: Frisco, Oostende
Book design: Style, Hulshout
Print: Flin Graphic Group, Oostkamp

© 2011 VUBPRESS Brussels University Press
VUBPRESS is an imprint of ASP nv (Academic and Scientific Publishers nv)
Ravensteingalerij 28
B-1000 Brussels
Tel. + 32 (0)2 289 26 50
Fax + 32 (0)2 289 26 59
E-mail info@vubpress.be
www.vubpress.be

ISBN 978 90 5487 909 1
NUR 782
Legal Deposit D/2011/11.161/072

Contents

Preface

The first edition of this book (2008) grew out of my yearly updated course text I had been using since 1996 to teach managerial economics of non-profit organisations at the Vrije Universiteit Brussel to last year undergraduate students and first year master students in (applied) economics and business. The yearly updating being a good example of incrementalism, and therefore a not so good example of rational textbook writing, forced me to restructure and rewrite the original text. When preparing the second edition, I took the opportunity to include new research insights, as well as to clarify a number of points that seemed confusing, and to correct a few errors.

Given the fact that economics are the scientific foundation of the present text (see Chapter 1 for an elaboration on this), its 'ideal' reader combines the following characteristics: apart from a genuine interest in the economics of the functioning of non-profit organisations, she has a good knowledge of basic microeconomics, knows standard algebra and the traditional mathematical optimisation techniques (including the use of Lagrangians), and is acquainted with the essential concepts of management and its most important functional domains such as strategic management, marketing, accounting, and finance. The level of the book is basic/intermediate, which sometimes required simplification of the theories presented. An attempt is made to be coherent throughout the book as to the use of symbols, implying that they frequently differ from the symbols used in the papers discussed. In the main text, mathematics are kept to a necessary minimum, more elaborate proofs being transferred to the appendices. Finally, without any conscious reason, managers will be female throughout the book, whereas all other persons interacting with them will be male, making the descriptions of these interactions more unambiguous.

Finally, non-native English speakers are always confronted with the fact that there is no such language as English, but different languages that are all called 'English'. In an attempt to write in a consistent way, I followed the UK version as shown on the *Cambridge Dictionaries Online*.

Acknowledgements

Though the writing of a book like this takes place in physical isolation, it would be impossible without a multitude of intellectual, logistic, and relational ties.

As far as my intellectual indebtedness is concerned, it is only fair to thank everybody who participated with me in researching the functioning of non-profit organisations, making it intellectually possible to produce this book. As it is impossible to rank the contribution of each of them, I present their names alphabetically according to their first names, as these are the names we use, sometimes even forgetting last names: Bruno Heyndels, Carine Smolders, Catherine Schepers, Chris Houtman, Cind Du Bois, Gert Huybrechts, Ilse Verschueren, Jemima Bidee, Jurgen Willems, Lore Wellens, Ralf Caers, Rein De Cooman, Roland Pepermans, Sara De Gieter, Stijn Van Puyvelde, and Tim Vantilborgh. Bruno, Cind, Ralf and Roland additionally contributed by commenting on a number or all drafts of the different chapters of this book. Also both the anonymous referees asked by Routledge to assess the first edition's proposal made valuable suggestions, most of which were eventually taken into account. I am also grateful to Routledge for having returned the rights to me, allowing me to publish this second edition with another publisher, and critical students at the Vrije Universiteit Brussel who incited me to rethink some passages of the first edition.

In terms of establishing a research network on non-profit organisation management and being enabled to discuss the latest contributions in the field, the biannial workshops organised by the European Institute for Advanced Studies in Management, which I had the pleasure to co-chair with Bernd Helmig, Fabrizio Panozzo, Irvine Lapsley, Nathalie Angelé-Halgand, and Noel Hyndman, were also very important, and shaped my thinking on this book's main topics. Editing with them the ensuing publications substantially added to this.

Mia Hofman was indispensable when it came to transform confusing drawings into clear and understandable figures, but even more as the psychological head of our department, keeping everybody as happy as possible, enabling all of us to maximally concentrate on our research, a role the importance of which cannot be overestimated.

Finally, I owe most to my parents, Micheline Churlet and Pierre Jegers, without who it would have been impossible to be were I am now, and my partner in life, Christine Locus, who makes me stay there.

List of frequently used symbols

Variables

π	outcome
Π	profit
a	altruism parameter
A	administrative costs net of fundraising costs
b	bonus
C	cost function $(= F_x + V)$
d	discretionary expenses
D	debt
e	effort
E(.)	expected value operator
Eq	equity
f	fundraising efforts
F	funds raised
F_x	fixed (production) cost
g	'warm glow' parameter
nW	non-monetary advantages
oo	organisational objectives
p	input price
P	output price
q	output quality
r	discount rate
R	revenues other than subsidies and fundraising revenues
S	subsidies

t	tax rate
TA	total assets (= D + Eq)
u	consumer utility
u_s	societal utility
U	utility (except societal utility and consumer utility)
V	total variable (production) cost
w	wage
W	wealth
y	output in units

Subscripts, superscripts

*	optimal value
a	of an agent
b	of a board member
d	of a donor
e	of an entrepreneur
em	of an entrepreneur-manager
f	of the founder
m	of a manager
max	maximal value
min	minimal value
np	of a non-profit organisation
p	of a profit organisation
w	of the workforce

1   Introduction

The focus of this book is on the economics of non-profit organisations' management. The social and economic roles of non-profit organisations all over the world are obvious, as becomes visible from the historical overview of the non-profit sector in the West by Robbins (2006) and in the US by Hall (2006), and from the description of the current position of non-profit organisations in a sample of 35 economically and socially very diverse countries by Anheier and Salamon (2006).[1] As the way non-profit organisations are managed impacts on their functioning, non-profit management is important when it comes to make the organisation's social and economic roles maximally operational.

In non-profit research, managerial topics are prominently present, but their economic foundations (the economics of management or 'managerial economics') are often ignored or neglected, as witnessed by their absence in the authoritative Research Handbooks edited by Powell (1987) and Powell and Steinberg (2006), who even 'consciously exclude ... chapters on the management of non-profit organisations' (Powell and Steinberg 2006: 9). Furthermore, neither management nor managerial economics show up in the list of topics predicted to be included in their Research Handbook's next editions (*ibid.*: ix).

Given the availability of numerous practitioner oriented texts on the management of non-profit organisations, there seems no need to increase their number with another one. The situation for managerial economic textbooks dealing with non-profit organisations is totally opposite: apparently, and somewhat surprisingly, in 2008 (when publishing the first edition of this book) their number was exactly zero. It is hoped that this number has increased to one by the publication of the present work. Though its title, *Managerial Economics of Non-Profit Organisations*, is self-explaining, an alternative title might have been *Theory of the Non-Profit Organisation*, mirroring the traditional 'theory of the firm' denomination of the managerial economic approach to profit

---

1   See also Boris and Steuerle (2006) for the situation in the US.

organisations, but being less clear for a potential readership not familiar with this body of theories.

An attempt has been made to integrate as much as possible the bits and pieces of high level economic work scattered around in a wide diversity of academic publications, as reflected by the list of references, to arrive at a coherent treatment of all the topics relevant for understanding non-profit organisations' management. The focus is on economic theory, but wherever possible theoretical insights are confronted with the available empirical evidence. This procedure has led to a book that could be labelled unbalanced, both with respect to the space devoted to the different topics as to the empirical evidence, most of which is US based and/or relates to health care industries. This lack of balance exactly reflects the status of the literature, and in that way shows in which domains further managerial economic research might be useful, though it will also become clear that on almost no managerial economic topic for non-profit organisations a generally accepted theoretical framework has emerged yet.

The next chapters, excluding the concluding one, can be grouped under three headings: definitions, the economic rationale of non-profit organisations and its implications on their functioning, and the economics of non-profit management.

The first group in fact consists of one chapter (Chapter 2). After having described the generic institutional forms under which goods or services can be produced (governments (at different levels), profit organisations, and non-profit organisations), and having elaborated on real life organisational forms, the definition of a non-profit organisation used throughout this book is presented: an organisation of which the founders or others are not entitled to (a part of) the organisation's profits, a condition traditionally called the non-distribution constraint (Hansmann 1987: 28). This definition is a purely economics based definition, which is justified by the fact that this book concentrates on what economic theory can teach on the functioning of non-profit organisations. It goes without saying that other approaches (such as from sociology, law, psychology, or organisation sciences) are equally valuable, and that these complement an economic approach of non-profit organisations.

Two aspects of the Hansmann definition are crucial in an economic analysis: organisational objectives, and incentive mechanisms with the ensuing efficiency consequences. Both are discussed, before closing the chapter with a section on a number of taxonomies of non-profit organisations.

In the second group of chapters economic justifications of the existence of non-profit organisations are presented. Chapter 3 is on the 'demand' for non-profit organisations, and Chapters 4 and 5 on the 'supply' of them. First, in Chapter 3, a fundamental economic reasoning on institutional choice is presented: the transaction cost theory, rooted in work by Coase (1937). Its prediction, if not its prescription, is that only institutions that minimise transaction costs can survive. Non-profit organisations are then compared to profit organisations from this perspective, which in fact amounts to translating the different forms of market failure known from the literature in a transaction cost language. Government failure theories are instrumental in comparing non-profit organisations with public bodies. Finally, industries in which at least two of the institutional forms coexist ('mixed' industries) need some explanation, as such a situation seems contrary to the idea that there is always one optimal institutional form for each transaction.

After having described why non-profit organisations might be viable, even in market oriented economies, the question why such organisations are established is discussed in the Chapters 4 and 5. The first of these concentrates on 'simple' organisations, whose activities are under control of the founder (also being the manager), whereas the last considers more complex organisations. The simple organisations can be characterised by a founder modelled as a non-profit entrepreneur. Under some circumstances, even an entrepreneur who is not altruistic can be shown to 'supply' a non-profit organisation. A specific model including both an entrepreneur-manager and subordinate staff is also discussed in Chapter 4.

An economic analysis of complex organisations is traditionally and fruitfully framed within the confines of a principal-agent approach. Therefore, its usefulness for specifically analysing complex non-profit organisations is the first topic dealt with in Chapter 5. Then, principals are discussed. In most analyses, the board is assumed to perform the principal's role: the effect of the composition of the board on organisational behaviour and more generally the functioning of the board are therefore discussed, before other possible principals (theoretically, every stakeholder can be a principal) are presented. The most frequently researched agent in non-profit organisations is the manager, to whom Chapter 5 devotes appropriate attention, including theory and (non-)practice of performance based remuneration systems for managers. Other agents comprise non-managerial staff members, who are also discussed. Finally, some agency based theoretical insights on agent selection close the section on agents. The chapter's last section turns the attention to volunteers and their place in principal-agent theorising on non-profit organisations.

In the last group of chapters the economics of a number of functional managerial domains are discussed through the lens of non-profit organisations, acknowledging the fact that management of non-profit organisations is 'a variant of the basic management model' (Newman and Wallender 1978: 31), and not something completely different. Therefore, the focus will be on the idiosyncrasies of non-profit organisations.

Strategic management is elaborated on in Chapter 6. First, strategic planning and strategic choices in non-profit organisations are discussed, and then some models designed to predict differences in strategic responses to exogenous shocks between non-profit organisations and profit organisations are presented, as well as a model on profit/non-profit competition in a mixed industry. The chapter ends with a short discussion of strategic differences between public providers and non-profit organisations.

The next chapter deals with marketing for non-profit organisations. After discussing the role of marketing management in non-profit organisations, the economics of four specific marketing domains are analysed: pricing, the role of volunteers, subsidies and gifts (both by individuals and by corporations), and the development of profit activities by non-profit organisations.

Chapter 8 is devoted to non-profit accounting and auditing. Although it is argued that the accounting and audit principles are not different from the principles to be applied in profit firms, understanding the presence and implementation of accounting and auditing in a non-profit context is different. A principal-agent based ('accounting and economics') theory is presented, in which non-profit specificities are taken into consideration, including the problem of (the lack of) accounting knowledge of board members and non-profit staff, and the question of non-profit organisations' compliance to accounting regulations. Specific cost accounting issues are also discussed, and economic analyses of accounting choices in financial accounting and cost accounting are presented.

The last chapter in this group of chapters deals with non-profit financial management, the economics of which are partly related to the standard financial theory, but also depart from it in a number of crucial respects. The topics analysed are the different sources of funds available for non-profit organisations, the determination of the cost of capital (and its impact on investment analysis), the ensuing insights on capital structure, and, finally, a discussion on the measurement of a non-profit organisation's financial vulnerability.

2 Defining non-profit organisations

Introduction

In this chapter an economics based definition of non-profit organisations is presented, building on traditional institutional ideas about the way goods and services can be provided. The non-profit organisation is described as one of the generic organisational forms, together with profit organisations and governmental bodies. Its specificity is the fact that financial surpluses, if present, cannot be distributed to owners, directors, and/or staff, making the group of non-profit organisations very diverse as to possible objectives, and possibly vulnerable because of the absence of financial incentives to run them in an efficient way.

The chapter concludes with a section on how to categorise non-profit organisations.

The provision of goods and services

Generic organisational forms

Except in very primitive societies, the production of a substantial part of goods and services (defined to include the promotion of ideas, ideologies or religions) is taken care of by formalised entities. These can be public or private.

The public sector is governed by its own set of decision rules and mechanisms, which are studied from a microeconomic point of view in the research field called *public choice*.[1] Clearly, the role of the public sector goes beyond producing goods and services, and includes domains such as macroeconomic policy, income redistribution, and fiscal policy.

The group of privately established organisations is very diverse. A fundamental divide is that between organisations allowing individuals to increase their financial wealth out of the organisation's profits, and other

---

1   Mueller (2003) is a leading textbook.

organisations. The first group is called the group of profit organisations, of which the microeconomic theory of their functioning can be found in, for example, Milgrom and Roberts (1992). Logically, the second group (also called the *third sector*, but other more or less accurate denominations exist (Salamon and Anheier 1992a: 128)) consists of non-profit organisations.

This brings us to three generic organisational forms: governments (at different levels), profit organisations, and non-profit organisations (Figure 2.1).

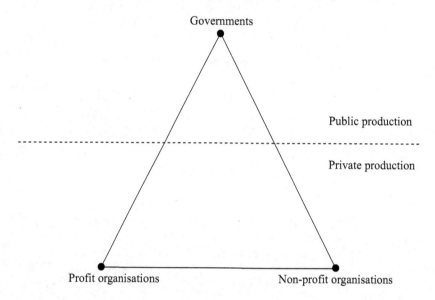

Figure 2.1   Generic organisational forms

Most of the economic analyses of organisational behaviour pertain to these generic or pure institutional forms, a position also taken in this book, with some exceptions. It goes without saying that in reality, organisational forms are frequently more complex (Weisbrod 1988: 1).

Real organisational forms

Figure 2.2 gives an (admittedly stylised) idea of how we might characterise real life organisations at a given moment in time. There is no reason to assume these characterisations should be static.

Organisation A in Figure 2.2 could be a privately founded non-profit organisation subsidised by a government (Salamon 1987). The fact that it receives a subsidy makes it (in a more or less limited way) subordinate to the subsidising authority, as the latter might force the organisation to behave in a way different from the way it would behave without receiving subsidies. B is an example of a legally private non-profit organisation founded and subsidised by a public authority, and C is an example of a profit firm owned by a government. A foundation owned and possibly funded by a profit firm, or an organisation grouping firms of the same industry, can be represented by the point D, and by E if it is subsidised. Note that organisations A, B, D, and E would be called *bureaus* by Niskanen (1971: 15), who defines them as organisations subject to the non-distribution constraint, earning part of their revenues from other sources than sales.

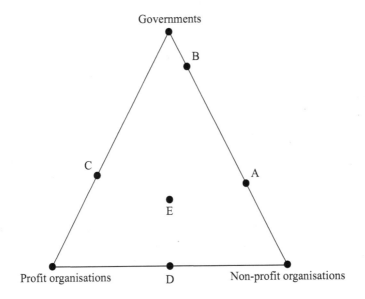

Figure 2.2 Real organisational forms

The fact that most real life organisations are mixtures of generic institutional forms implies that if one wants to assess the practical implications for organisational behaviour of theoretical predictions, one has to take into consideration two or three bodies of research, not always mutually consistent, weighing the profit, non-profit, and public characteristics of the organisations under study.

A frequently observed and researched organisational form is the social enterprise. Numerous definitions exist, but they all transgress the differences between profit-organisations and non-profit organisations by focusing on organisational objectives, such as in the definition provided by Young (2009: 23): '[s]ocial enterprise is activity intended to address social goals through the operation of private organisations in the marketplace.' Examples of social enterprises falling outside the scope of non-profit organisations are cooperatives and some kinds of institutions providing job training or fostering social integration by employing some specifically targeted categories of people.

Definition

The previous section implies the following definition of a non-profit organisation: an organisation whose owners, directors, and/or staff are not entitled to (a part of) the organisation's profits, a condition traditionally called the *non-distribution constraint* (Hansmann 1987: 28).

Though for economic analysis this definition is sufficient, and conveniently parsimonious, more elaborate alternatives also appear in the literature, leading Anheier to say that 'definitions are perhaps the most lamented and frequently misunderstood "deficit" in our field' (Anheier 1995: 16). A definition frequently encountered is the structural-operational one by Salamon and Anheier (1992a: 135): a non-profit organisation should be formal, private, self-governing, voluntary (in membership and participation), and satisfying the non-distribution constraint. Apart from the involvement of volunteers, there is no conceptual difference with the definition above, as using the term 'organisation' implies it is formal, private and self-governing. Needless to say, a large number of non-profit organisations lean on volunteers, but surely not all of them. This might explain why the United Nations makes no reference to volunteers in its definition of a non-profit organisation: an organisation that is self-governing, institutionally separate from government, non-compulsory, and that meets the non-distribution constraint (United Nations 2003: 17).

Morris (2000: 39-41) seems to define the non-profit sector more in terms of activities and social outcomes, including in the sector, for example, mutual-aid societies and cooperatives, which do not meet the structural-operational definition of non-profit organisations, let alone the non-distribution constraint. But this does not seem to be an appropriate critique on the definition of a non-profit organisation as such, but only illustrates the difference between the group of non-profit organisations and the larger group of civil society institutions, as in fact Morris herself rightly points out (Morris 2000: 41).

Therefore, there seems to be no reason to depart from the non-distribution constraint characterisation of non-profit organisations. Notice that this does not imply that non-profit organisations are barred from making profits, or that they are forbidden to employ paid staff. The point is that profits cannot be distributed, not to owners, board members, or staff, making profit based wage schemes incompatible with the non-profit status of the organisation (see also Chapter 5).

Finally, note that legal or administrative conditions, such as registration under the US Internal Revenue Service articles 501(c)(3) or (4), are just that: legal and administrative conditions, adding nothing to a definition suitable for economic analysis (Smith and Shen 1996: 271).

Organisational objectives

As there is no point in establishing an organisation with the sole objective of not distributing profits, one might wonder how non-profit organisations' objectives can be modelled to allow a meaningful economic analysis, comparable to the role of profit maximisation in the *theory of the firm* literature. The non-distribution constraint being a negative condition, its complement encompasses all kinds of possible objectives, a number of which might even be morally reprehensible (depending on who's point of view is taken), totally unrelated to each other, or contradictory. Therefore, it seems inevitable that 'there is no consensus among economists regarding the objective function of npos' (Schiff and Weisbrod 1991: 621), or that finding some overall objective function for non-profit organisations is impossible (Kanter and Summers 1987: 155). At a general level, it can only be said that these objectives should reflect in one way or another the incentives experienced by persons involved in establishing and running the non-profit organisations (Valentinov 2008b: 40-41; see also Chapters 4 and 5).

In economic terms, organisational objectives will be reflected by the organisational utility function, U_{npo}. Different variables have been put forward to serve as its main arguments. Output quantity and output quality go back to Newhouse (1970), with all kinds of variations such as an 'optimal' relation between them, trading off for example the quality of education and the number of students reached (Steinberg 1986a: 508), or artistic quality and the size of audiences (DiMaggio 1987: 206). Cleveland and Krashinksy (2009) however point out, in an empirical study on the Canadian child care market,[2] that quality strategies are only sustainable when the market can bear this ('thick' markets).

Another argument frequently found in non-profit utility functions is achieving zero profits, or the equivalent objective of covering all costs incurred, though this condition might also be considered a constraint under which organisational utility is maximised. Some final examples of arguments are cash-flows (Davis 1972: 1) or even profits (Brody 1996: 493), which are theoretically acceptable non-profit organisation's objectives as long as the non-distribution constraint is respected, welfare of (a part of) membership (Canning *et al.* 2003: 247) or clients (Handy and Webb 2003: 266).

As already noted by DiMaggio (1987: 209), organisational objectives cannot be expected to remain unchanged through time. Societal needs might evolve, new needs within the confines of the organisation's mission might emerge, and original objectives may be reached. Furthermore, contingent factors such as dimension or age of the organisation, socio-economic characteristics of sponsors, the volunteers/professionals mix within the organisation, subsidy regulations (see also Chapter 7), changing relations with governments, or competition from profit organisation and/or other non-profit organisations (Brickley and Van Horn 2002; Minkoff and Powell 2006: 592-594) could impact on them, though the last factors can also be considered an additional constraint on behaviour.

In spite of the idea that 'the objective function [of a non-profit organisation] is unobservable' (Pauly 1987: 258), Vitaliano (2003) is an example of an empirical investigation into non-profit organisations' objectives. For a sample of Medicaid residents of New York nursing homes, he distinguishes profit maximisers (characterised by a situation in which marginal costs equal marginal revenues) and utility maximisers (marginal costs higher than marginal revenues). Most organisations in this sample appeared to be profit maximisers,

---

2   325 child care classrooms in 1998.

but this might (at least partly) be explained by profit organisations' competition (see also Chapter 3). Another empirical, but rather indirect, strategy that may be used to identify organisational objectives is to analyse, if present, the incentive design of the remuneration packages for the organisation's top management (Ballou and Weisbrod 2003: 1898; see also Chapter 5), or to contrast behavioural implications of assumed non-profit objectives with behavioural implications of profit objectives or governmental objectives (Du Bois *et al.* 2004a). The work of Lindrooth and Weisbrod (2007) and Koning (2008) are examples of the latter. Lindrooth and Weisbrod (2007) compare admission policies of (religion based) non-profit hospices and profit maximising hospices, facing for the large majority of their residents the same financial incentives and also showing no other systematic differences affecting admission policies. The financial incentives make longer stays more profitable. Their sample consists of all Medicare reimbursed admissions to 638 US hospices between 1993 and 1996, and reveals that lengths of stay are significantly longer in the profit hospices, a situation not justified by treatment differences, but by policies aimed at attracting residents with the more 'profitable' diagnoses, implying longer lengths of stay (Lindrooth and Wiesbrod 2007: 353-355). This observation can be explained by the non-profit hospices caring more for all persons at the end of their lives, though it does not rule out an (in)efficiency explanation (*ibid.*: 347), which is spelled out in the next section. Koning (2008) compares selection behaviour by job training and mediation services in the Netherlands, both profit and non-profit.[3] In comparable situations, the profit providers seem to more severely select potential clients, but also manage to avoid more selected clients to drop out, as could be expected from the payment structure for such services. Taking all effects together, non-profit providers perform only marginally better than their profit counterparts in terms of eventual job placements (Koning 2008: 234-237).

To conclude this section, the paper by Gertler and Kuan (2009) may be referred to. They try to assess the value of non-profit objectives for the owners of non-profit organisations by comparing the prices paid by non-profit acquirers and by profit acquirers. In a sample of 135 hospital acquisitions (US, 1990-2000), they find that non-profit hospitals sold to non-profit organisations change ownership at a 43 per cent discount as compared to an acquisition by a profit organisation (Gertler and Kuan 2009: 301). The reason for this difference is the value attached by the sellers to the survival of their ideals.

Incentive implications: the property rights approach

When trying to understand organisational behaviour and the underlying incentives, the concepts of *residual control* and *residual claims* are essential. Both reflect a specific aspect of the exercise of property rights. Residual control can be defined as 'the right to make any decisions concerning the asset's use

---

3   Almost 1,500 contracts awarded in the period 2002-2005, of which 4 per cent for non-profit
     providers.

that are not explicitly controlled by law or assigned to another by contract' (Milgrom and Roberts 1992: 289), and a residual claim the fact to be 'entitled to receive any net income that the firm produces' (Milgrom and Roberts 1992: 291), net income in this context also being called *residual return,* or the income after having met all legal and contractual obligations. The interplay between the two is key to understand organisational incentives (*ibid.*), as had already been cogently argued by Alchian and Demsetz (1972).

As the owners of a non-profit organisation by (the non-distribution constraint) definition cannot be residual claimants of the organisation, they have no (financial) incentives to monitor closely the organisation's management and staff. Alchian and Demsetz (1972: 790) therefore predict to 'find greater shirking in non-profit ... enterprises', and consequently less efficiency as compared to profit organisations in the same market, if these are conceivable (Steinberg 1987: 128). Competition by profit organisations in the same market might mitigate efficiency losses (Feigenbaum 1987).

As will be shown in later chapters, the property rights view on non-profit (in)efficiency is an over-simplification at best. To give just some of the reasons for this: the motives of owners, managerial employees and non-managerial employees of non-profit organisations might significantly differ from the motives of their counterparts involved in profit organisations (Callen and Falk 1993: 51), or there might exist situations in which visibility or self-dealing compensate for an alleged inclination to inefficiency (Steinberg 1987: 127). The analytical paper by Gassler (1997) leads to a similar conclusion: 'the non-profit constraint does not cause inefficiency nearly to the extent that many economists seem to believe.' (Gassler 1997: 278).

As the proof of the pudding is in the eating, resorting to empirical studies might enable us to assess the merits of the efficiency implications derived from the property rights approach. Steinberg (2006: 128) refers to hundreds of studies on efficiency differences between profit organisations and non-profit organisations. The results go in all possible directions: no efficiency differences, non-profit organisations being more efficient, or non-profit organisations being less efficient (the majority of cases). But all these papers suffer from a number of methodological problems (*ibid.*), the most important being 'their failure to control adequately for varieties ... in quality and amenities' (Sloan 1988: 117), which is the consequence of the difficulties in defining non-profit organisations' objectives and measuring organisational performance directly and objectively in terms of these objectives. Selection bias (profit organisations serving client segments other than non-profit organisations) and the impact of competition (mentioned above) are additional problems not always dealt with in empirical efficiency comparisons between profit organisations and non-profit organisations (Kessler and McClellan 2002: 489). Finally, concentrating on output measures instead of process variables might distort the empirical findings, as illustrated by the work of Chesteen *et al.* (2005), and the same problem might be caused by inadequately taking into consideration the input of volunteers (Callen 1994: 215). To sum up, the empirical research to date cannot be considered to be conclusive as to this topic.

Classifying non-profit organisations

As is the case for profit organisations, non-profit organisations are not alike. A classification according to economically or otherwise significant criteria might prove useful (Salamon and Anheier 1992b: 268).

Hansmann (1987: 28) proposes a global classification according to two dimensions: donative non-profit organisations versus commercial non-profit organisations, and mutual non-profit organisations versus entrepreneurial non-profit organisations, leading to four groups. A donative non-profit organisation is funded mainly by donations and subsidies, a commercial one generates most of its funds by selling goods or services, though clients might be insured by public or private schemes (as is frequently the case in the health care sector). Mutual non-profit organisations are run by their funders, whereas entrepreneurial ones are not. Clearly, in the real world different kinds of mixed forms exist, but for the sake of theoretical argument this classification has proved to be very instrumental.

A special case of a donative non-profit organisation is the foundation, which can be defined as private capital to be used in the general interest (Anheier 2005: 51). Foundations already existed more than 2,000 years ago, under the ancient Greek and Roman republics (Prewitt 2006: 260-265).

Though other classification systems have been proposed (e.g. Douglas 1987: 51), the one put forward by Hansmann has gained wide, if not universal, acceptance. Note that this system does not take into account the activities performed by the organisations, and that the ensuing categories therefore cannot be considered to be industries. Different attempts have been made to construct a system of non-profit industries, such as the National Taxonomy of Exempt Entities drawn up by the National Center for Charitable Statistics in the United States, but one has to admit that these industries are not exclusive territories for non-profit organisations. Nursing homes, as an example, can be owned by profit organisations, public authorities, or non-profit organisations. Nevertheless, the United Nations commissioned the development of a non-profit organisations classification system, as a satellite account within the System of National Accounts, to the John Hopkins University Center for Civil Society. After testing in 13 countries all over the world, this resulted in the essentially activity based International Classification of Non-profit Organisations (ICNPO) (United Nations 2003: 27, 30). Its main structure is described in Table 2.1. Further details can be found in Appendix I.

Further refinements, both within and across (sub-)groups have been proposed, such as the distinction between multipurpose organisations, support and service organisations (including auxiliaries, councils, standard-setting and governance organisations), and other organisations (Salamon, Anheier 1992b: 289), or between member-serving and public-serving organisations (United Nations 2003: 32). Broadening the definitions to encompass all organisations in the *social economy*, including also mutual associations, cooperatives and social enterprises, is easily possible (*ibid.*).

Table 2.1 International classification of non-profit organizations: main groups and subgroups

Groups	Subgroups
1 Culture and recreation	1 100 Culture and arts 1 200 Sports 1 300 Other recreation and social clubs
2 Education and research	2 100 Primary and secondary education 2 200 Higher education 2 300 Other education 2 400 Research
3 Health	3 100 Hospitals and rehabilitation 3 200 Nursing homes 3 300 Mental health and crisis intervention 3 400 Other health services
4 Social services	4 100 Social services 4 200 Emergency and relief 4 300 Income support and maintenance
5 Environment	5 100 Environment 5 200 Animal protection
6 Development and housing	6 100 Economic, social and community development 6 200 Housing 6 300 Employment and training
7 Law, advocacy and politics	7 100 Civic and advocacy organizations 7 200 Law and legal services 7 300 Political organizations
8 Philanthropic intermediaries and voluntarism promotion	8 100 Grant-making foundations 8 200 Other philanthropic intermediaries and voluntarism promotion
9 International	9 100 International activities
10 Religion	10 100 Religious congregations and associations
11 Business and professional associations, unions	11 100 Business associations 11 200 Professional associations 11 300 Labour unions
12 Not elsewhere classified	12 100 Not elsewhere classified

Source: United Nations (2003: 31).

3   The demand for non-profit organisations

Introduction

In Chapter 2 the generic organisational forms were introduced, but the question why they exist and survive was not dealt with. In the present chapter it is argued that the fundamental answer lies in the cost implications of the institutional choice when governing economic transactions, the minimal cost bearing institution being theoretically the only viable one for a specific transaction.

Most of the relevant academic literature on the existence and survival of non-profit organisations, which is reviewed here, takes a comparative stance and analyses conditions under which non-profit organisations are 'better' than profit organisations, or conditions under which non-profit organisations are 'better' than public agencies. Though this seems to imply that there is always a 'best' institutional form for a given transaction, frequently two or three of them coexist. Theoretical reasons for this will be developed.

Institutional choice

From an economist's point of view, the fundamental answer to the question why non-profit organisations exist and survive goes back to Coase (1937), who argues that the transaction (a transfer between (at least) two parties of goods or services (Milgrom and Roberts 1992: 21)) is the core concept to be considered. Societal welfare under market governance of transactions is then compared to societal welfare under institutionalised governance. In situations where the latter exceeds the former, the formation of institutions is economically efficient, and their existence understandable. Though Coase contrasted the market with profit organisations, the same line of reasoning can be followed to differentiate institutional forms as to their welfare implications, resulting in a set of conditions and situations under which non-profit organisations can be expected to be welfare maximising. If we assume unrestrained and costless welfare transferability there would be no economic reason to establish another kind of organisation than the welfare maximising one (Krashinsky 1986: 129), but in reality this assumption is seldom met, implying surplus distribution might be a second factor to account for when explaining the demand for a given kind of organisations (Gui 1991: 555).

The traditional way to address the question why there is a demand for non-profit organisations consists in following an implicit hierarchy of institutions (Weisbrod 1988: 25). To govern a transaction, first try the market. If this does not work, try a profit organisation, after which possibly some public authority may be considered. And, as some kind of last resort, we still have the non-profit organisation (Young 2000: 150). Apart from the fact that this hierarchy is fully anti-chronological when looking at the first appearances of the different generic organisational forms (Krashinsky 1986: 114; Weisbrod 1988: 4), it also implies a negative justification of the existence of non-profit organisations: when everything else fails, try a non-profit organisation. A more neutral and positive approach is warranted (Clark 1980; Salamon and Anheier 1998: 225), in which the welfare implications of institutions are compared with one another, and in which therefore each organisational form can 'fail', hence the denomination 'a three failures approach' (Steinberg 2006: 119). These failures can be time and location specific, as can be the ensuing rankings of governance structures according to their welfare implications (Ben-Ner 2002).

The transaction cost approach

Transaction costs

Besides the (utility) benefits accruing to the parties involved and the production costs, which we will assume for the ease of exposition not to be affected by the governance structure in place, transactions engender supplementary costs (*transaction costs*), at least in welfare terms. They stem from the *bounded rationality* of the parties involved in the transaction, and possible opportunistic behaviour of these parties.

Bounded rationality involves two aspects. The parties do not know all the characteristics of the transaction relevant to gauge perfectly its welfare implications (imperfect and incomplete information), and even if they knew these, their information processing capacities do not allow them to combine these characteristics logically in a way leading to optimal decision making.

In the words of Williamson (1979: 239), in transaction cost theory 'economic agents are permitted to ... mislead, disguise, obfuscate, and confuse'. This kind of behaviour is called opportunistic behaviour, a kind of behaviour which, for the sake of realism, cannot be excluded. A typical situation allowing such behaviour is a situation characterised by informational asymmetries, in which the better informed party can misuse his informational advantage.

Transaction cost thinking distinguishes three transaction characteristics impacting on transaction costs: asset specificity, frequency, and *ex-ante* uncertainty with respect to the efforts required by the parties involved to meet the terms of the transaction and to the (utility effects of the) outcome itself.

According to Williamson (1991: 281) *asset specificity* is the most prominent one. Asset specificity is defined as the lack of reusability of investments explicitly geared towards a specific transaction. Different forms of asset specificity can be observed. They include location specificity (e.g. when a supplier invests near to his only or main client), physical specificity (e.g. installing production capacity that is useful for one specific client only), human asset specificity (e.g. establishing relationships with specific clients, or employees following courses only useful when staying with their current employer), brand specificity (e.g. an actor being identified with a popular character, making it impossible for him to play any other role in a convincing way (Acs and Gerlowski 1996: 152)), and allocative specificity (losing the possibility to employ the resources invested in another way). Clearly, higher specificity invites more opportunistic behaviour by the party enjoying the assets (the 'hold up' problem).

The, *ceteris paribus*, effect of frequency on transaction costs is straightforward: more frequent transactions can lead to higher transaction costs, almost by definition.

The *ex-ante* uncertainty surrounding the transaction with respect to the efforts required by the parties involved to meet its terms and to the (utility effects of the) outcome itself might incite some of the opportunistic parties involved in the transaction to reduce their efforts or lower the quality produced, higher uncertainty leading to higher expected transaction costs, again *ceteris paribus*.

In what follows, we will confine ourselves to the choice between institutional forms, but a transaction cost based analysis can also be made at the transaction level itself. An example of this in a non-profit context is the paper by Thornton (2010), who explains the presence of restricions on grants donated by charitable foundations to non-profit organisations. Based on data on 2,510 grants received by 2,112 organisations from 556 foundations,[1] they conclude that '[m]ore restrictive contracts are offered as output becomes increasingly contractible or as the potential for *ex-post* opportunism rises' (Thornton 2010: 52), which matches exactly what is predicted by transaction cost theory.

Understanding the existence of non-profit organisations

Once a potential transaction has been selected, benefits, production costs and transaction costs can, theoretically, be identified. Ideally (under the assumption of costless welfare transferability), the aggregate level of all costs to all parties affected should guide the choice of an optimal governance institution, but mostly only the benefits and costs of the individual parties directly involved in the transaction will help us understand why in some circumstances non-profits seem to be needed, or why federations of non-profit organisations emerge (Young and Faulk 2010).

Unfortunately, to date no comprehensive theory has been developed to fully explain the demand for non-profit organisations. The insights presented

---

1   US, data relating to the year 2000.

below were developed in comparative independence from one another, are not mutually exclusive, and do not encompass all types of non-profit organisations. Nevertheless, most of them build on an implicit or explicit transaction cost way of thinking (Holtmann and Ullmann 1991; Valentinov 2006, 2007), some of then concentrating more on aspects of opportunism, others on information asymmetries and the bounded rationality of the agents involved (Valentinov 2007: 53).

Non-profit organisations versus profit organisations

'Market failure' theories

In line with the traditional institutional hierarchy described earlier in this chapter, this group of theories explains the need for non-profit organisations by looking for circumstances in which 'the market' fails. Though in Coasian terms a market transaction should be defined as a transaction between independent individuals, its generally accepted interpretation in the present context is the provision of a good or service by a profit organisation. Market failure can be defined as a situation in which the market fails to reach optimal welfare levels or welfare allocations. A specific case in point is the failure to provide some good or services.

As noted by Hansmann (1980: 61), we may not forget that the market can be very successful under a large variety of conditions which can be traced back to conditions leading to low transaction costs: low uncertainty (buyers have a correct *ex-ante* view on quality and prices, unambiguous contracts), limited incentives for opportunistic behaviour due to the existence of objective *ex-post* quality measures and efficient enforcement procedures (for example by competent courts). A number of the market failures described in the literature deal with some departures from these conditions.

The market failing to provide some goods or services

Contract failure

Some transactions (e.g. surgery, education) are so complex that it is economically unfeasble to write a watertight contract dealing with all the possible outcomes of the process. Incomplete contracts are the result, as well as uncertainty with respect to the outcomes of the transaction. In situations where the outcome is very important for one of the parties involved, and in which this party faces an informational disadvantage, profit maximising providers might be (assumed to be) inclined towards opportunistic behaviour, exerting less effort and producing lower quality. The expected transaction costs to be borne by the consumer can reach such a level that he might prefer not to enter into the transaction at all. Hansmann (1980) is credited for having proposed the idea that the non-distribution constraint would mitigate or even destroy this suspicion of opportunism, making this kind of transactions possible, though Arrow (1963), almost twenty years before Hansmann (1980), implicitly makes the same point with respect to medical treatments: '[a]s a signal to the buyer of his intentions to act as thoroughly in the buyer's behalf as possible, the physician avoids the obvious stigmata of profit-maximising.' (*ibid.*: 965). Fama and Jensen (1983b: 342) develop the same line of reasoning with respect to charities. In the words of Steinberg and Gray (1993: 306) this goes as follows: '[i]It is difficult to conceive of a type of transaction that has more contract failure potential than one in which party A provides services to party B for which party C is expected to pay'.

There have been a number of interesting and challenging attempts to show formally that, from a social welfare point of view, non-profit organisations are optimal in situations of informational asymmetry, unfortunately under rather artificial assumptions (Chillemi and Gui 1991; Easley and O'Hara 1983, 1988). Furthermore, these models do not analyse contract failure as such, but compare welfare outcomes of the provision of profit organisations and non-profit organisations respectively.

It is fair to say that the contract failure reasoning is still a 'dominant rationale' in non-profit organisation theory (Ortmann and Schlesinger 1997: 98), in spite of the fact that a number of conditions must be met in order to explain the existence of non-profit organisations by the presence of information asymmetries (*ibid.*): there are no reputation effects in favor of profit organisations, the people in charge of the non-profit organisations must be trustworthy, implying that these organisations must take care not to attract staff with opportunistic motives (the 'adulteration challenge').

Being a dominant rationale does not exclude the fact that it has been criticized by a number of authors. Brody (1996: 524) notes that production by profit organisations under information asymmetry is possible if non-profit watchdogs can divulge the information necessary to bridge information gaps, especially when applying modern information technologies. One could respond by saying that a non-profit organisation is still needed, albeit in a different, modern, configuration, and that this need is still the consequence of information asymmetry and the concomitant impossibility of writing complete contracts. The fact that a large number of health care professionals are employed in profit hospitals and that a number of them are or were paid in a fee for service system does not support the contract failure theory either (Brody 1996: 463, n21; Sloan 1988: 109). But also in the health care sector a variety of non-profit and/or public monitoring agencies, standard-setting bodies, or patient organisations exist, indirectly confirming the main insight of the contract failure approach: the need for non-profit organisations when confronted with information asymmetry for major transactions.

There is also empirical support at least for the basic assumptions of the contract failure theory. Chou (2002),[2] applying subtle econometric techniques, finds that in nursing homes where information asymmetries can be observed (for example by looking at visit frequencies), profit nursing homes' quality

---

2   2,992 elderly people admitted to 1,887 US nursing homes (1984-1994).

was lower than that of non-profit nursing homes. The paper by Grabowski and Hirth (2003) takes a comparable perspective. They assess two relationships,[3] the first between non-profit nursing homes market shares and profit nursing homes' quality, and the second between non-profit nursing homes market shares and average market quality. Both are significantly positive, implying that the presence of non-profit nursing homes is socially useful, as less informed clients will resort to non-profit homes, and profit homes will provide a higher quality service (*ibid.*: 3).

Both these studies look at the supply side of the contract failure story, but there is also a demand side aspect, at least in mixed markets where both institutional forms are present, but also when there are only non-profit organisations in the market. If potential clients do not know whether organisations are profit or non-profit, or if they do not put more trust in non-profit organisations than in profit organisations, or if the market is segmented along the profit/non-profit divide, the contract failure justification of the existence of non-profit organisations has no ground in markets in which profit organisations compete with non-profit organisations (Ortmann and Schlesinger 1997: 107), and, logically, not even in pure non-profit markets. Schlesinger *et al.* (2004) address this question by surveying 5,000 US citizens on their perceptions of profit organisations and non-profit organisations in the hospital and insurance industries. About one third of the respondents did not know the difference between profit organisations and non-profit organisations (*ibid.*: 689). The remaining respondents had a positive perception in favour of non-profit organisations as far as non-discrimination and reliability were concerned, but a negative perception on non-profit quality compared with profit quality (*ibid.*: 692). Ballou (2005) investigates a comparable question on nursing homes.[4] He concludes that 'ownership type does appear to matter to consumers', with 'consistently positive non-profit effects' (*ibid.*: 253), which he ascribes to perceived quality differences.

All in all, these results, which are geographically and temporally very partial anyway, do not lead to the conclusion that the contract failure approach of the existence of non-profit organisations lost all credibility.

Public goods

Public goods (including here public services) are goods available for any consumer (*non-excludability*), and their consumption by one consumer does not prevent consumption by another (*non-rivalry*). Classic examples are the army, fire brigades, lighthouses, education, health care, museums, or public transport systems, though not all of them are pure public goods, mostly due to capacity constraints barring or delaying consumption (*congestion goods*) (Maddison and Foster 2003) or entrance fees (*toll goods*) (Young and Steinberg 1995: 192).

(Pure) public goods are, almost by definition, an open invitation for opportunistic behaviour by consumers, making monetary revenues very

---

3   16,978 US nursing homes (1995-1996).
4   3,605 observations for the 1984-1995 period (Wisconsin (US)).

uncertain. Furthermore, a substantial number of the public goods we know require very specific investments, making them unattractive for profit organisations to produce. Hence a market failure, and a rationale for non-profit organisations to provide these goods, even in cases when they are not fully public, as in the examples mentioned above (Chang and Tuckman 1996: 27).

Client control

Organisations in which the members want full control over activities are not easily found in the market. Leisure organisations (such as the 'country clubs' in the US) and a number of mutual organisations are examples. One could argue that the need for non-profit organisations to cope with this demand is just a special case of contract failure, but this is not entirely true (Hansmann 1987: 33). Even in cases where other institutions could provide exactly the goods or services wanted, the members further increase their transaction related utility because of having control in their 'own' organisation.

Advocacy

Promoting ideas and convincing other people are transactions for which *a priori* there are no consumers, and certainly no consumers who are willing to exchange something of value to be elected to receive these ideas. It is therefore not surprising that we will not find profit organisations promoting ideological, religious or political ideas, though there are people who want these ideas to be promoted. This is a special kind of market failure, and these people can remedy the failure by establishing their own organisations which we could label supplier induced. Given the specific characteristics of the transactions involved, these organisations can only be non-profit organisations.

The market failing to reach optimal welfare levels or welfare allocations

Unwanted welfare outcomes

If legally allowed, the market can provide an amount of goods and services that show characteristics of both private goods and public goods, *quasi public goods* (Anheier 2005: 118), such as the congestion goods or toll goods mentioned earlier. The profit motive can lead to problems of accessibility, resulting in a social welfare loss. In that sense the market can also be judged to fail, essentially because of undersupply. Non-profit organisations can substitute for the absent market.

Transactions in which contract failures arise can also possibly be governed by markets, as long as the transaction costs surrounding the transaction are in one way or another more than compensated by the perceived revenues. This does not imply that there are no welfare improvement possibilities. The same transaction governed by a non-profit organisation might reduce, for instance, the uncertainty perceived by one of the parties involved, decreasing the transaction costs, and increasing welfare.

For both cases, the central idea is that the non-distribution constraint implies incentives for the producer of the goods or services not to behave opportunistically.

Stochastic demand

An interesting contribution towards explaining the existence of non-profit organisations is made by Holtmann (1983). In a complicated model, he compares the effect on total welfare of profit production versus non-profit production in the case of a stochastic demand. Firms decide on price and capacity. Non-profit firms (defined as firms not requiring any return on net assets) are shown to generate more welfare. As stochastic demand is central in this model, it neatly fits in the transaction cost approach, as the effects of a kind of uncertainty are assessed.

Employee motives

Francois' model (2001), inspired by Glaeser and Shleifer (1998), to explain the existence of non-profit organisations, explicitly discards the problem of non-contractibility of output, but concentrates on the employees of profit organisations and non-profit organisations (see also Chapters 4 and 5 on this). He assumes identical utility functions for each member of society, be it an owner of a profit firm, a founder of a non-profit organisation, or an employee of one of either kind of organisation. This utility function contains an argument reflecting concern for the organisation's output, called 'care' by the author. Output is perfectly contractible by the government, so contract failure is not an issue here. For goods or services inducing a high amount of concern, such as health care or education, the non-distribution constraint results, admittedly through a rather artificial mechanism, in non-profit organisations producing at a lower cost than profit organisations, with obvious welfare implications. Note that this effect stems from the production costs being affected by governance structures, and not the transaction costs as such.

Presence of both profit organisations and non-profit organisations on the same markets

The previous sections might give the impression that the choice between a profit organisation and a non-profit organisation to govern a given transaction leads to just one of of them being optimal. In reality, different markets exist in which the two kinds of organisations coexist. Typical examples of such mixed industries are the US hospital industry, the Canadian child care market (Cleveland and Krashinksy 2009), or the nursing home industry in a number of European countries. Mostly, these markets also contain a more or less substantial public component. Reviewing a rather old literature on the market shares of non-profit organisations in such markets, Brown and Slivinski (2006: 152) conclude that these are higher when the tax advantage of being a non-profit organisation increases and when the undersupply problem already mentioned is more severe, and lower when the markets grow faster. They also discuss possible reasons why in mixed industries non-profit organisations might want to convert to a profit status: survival, a way of cashing in profits which are now retained within the non-profit organisation, getting easier access to capital markets, and a reaction to increasing risk due to changing regulations, making more risk-averse managers of non-profit organisations less motivated to manage (*ibid.*: 154).

A possible explanation for the existence of mixed industries might consist in noticing that the theories mentioned above are normative, but that opportunism or bounded rationality prevent the optimal situation from prevailing.

However, other explanations might be put forward, less pessimistic as to human nature. What is perceived to be one market might conceal a segmented market: 'when proprietary firms coexist with public or non-profit providers, there are systematic differences in the form or quality of outputs or the way they are distributed to consumers' (Weisbrod 1988: 40). Market failure could be present in one segment (for example the segment with less informed potential clients), but not in the other (Hansmann 1987: 31).

The model by Holtmann and Ullmann (1991) conveys the same idea. Although it was designed to understand the situation on the nursing home market, it is easily generalised for other markets. Assume a consumer has a non-mutually exclusive choice between a quantity y_p provided by a profit organisation, and a quantity y_{np} produced by a non-profit organisation. The product or service quality q_{np} provided by the non-profit organisation is not subject to uncertainty ($q_{np} = y_{np}$), whereas the quality provided by the profit organisation is stochastic ($\tilde{q}_p = \tilde{z}y_p$, with $E(\tilde{z}) = 1$). The consumer is a utility maximizer:

$$\text{Max} \quad E(u(\tilde{q}_p, q_{np}))$$
$$y_p, y_{np}$$

subject to the budget constraint $B = P_p y_p + P_{np} y_{np}$, where P_p and P_{np} are the output prices of profit producers and non-profit producers respectively.

In Figure 3.1 we can distinguish three possible cases, according to the position of the budget line and the shape of the indifference curves. When the utility function implies an indifference curve as u_1 (u_3), a utility maximizing consumer will resort exclusively to profit organisations (non-profit organisations). If the indifference curve resembles u_2, the consumer turns to both. This might explain the coexistence of profit organisations and non-profit organisations in the same market. Also assuming the consumers to be heterogeneous in terms of their utility functions, resulting in markets with 'u_1 consumers', 'u_2 consumers' and 'u_3 consumers', results in a comparable configuration of supply. Technically, even two of the three categories of consumers are sufficient for this result.

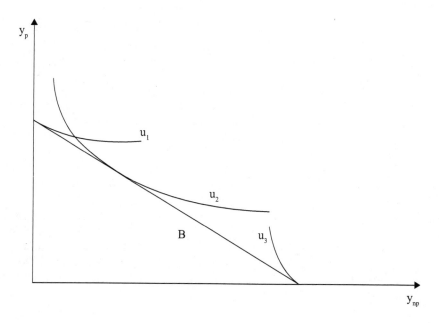

Figure 3.1 Profit organisations and non-profit organisations on the same market

Source: based on Holtmann and Ullmann (1991).

Handy's paper (1997) is comparable in its logic, and includes the public sector in its analysis. Trade-offs are not between two types of products, but between two product components (measurable and immeasurable, both of which are assumed to carry a price, a rather heroic assumption as to the immeasurable product component). Combining the fact that the slopes of the budget lines are affected by the institutional form of the producer and heterogeneous utility functions results also in an equilibrium characterised by the presence of profit organisations, non-profit organisations, and public organisations.

Three additional points can be raised as to the coexistence of profit organisations and non-profit organisations in the same market.

First, as already mentioned, both groups of organisations interact when simultaneously present in the same market. Although in Chapter 6 a theoretical model is presented confronting competitive strategies of profit organisations and non-profit organisations in the same industry, we can already refer to the research by Grabowski and Hirth mentioned above (2003) where it was observed that the presence of non-profit organisations in a market forced the competing profit organisations to increase their output quality.[5] Other interactions have also been observed such as the presence of profit organisations making their

---

5   See Thornton and Cave (2010: 236) for an example of the presence of profit organisations forcing non-profit organisations to improve quality, in a sample of 75 private foster care agencies in Kentucky (US) with data for 2005-2006.

non-profit competitors more efficient,[6] but also more profit oriented (Duggan 2002;[7] Horwitz and Nichols 2009).[8]

Second, exogenous pressures on the markets in which both kinds of organisations are present can be substantially more influential as to organisational strategies than institutional differences, as is illustrated by the results obtained by Skinner and Rosenberg (2006) in their qualitative research on the effects of the introduction of managed competition in rural Ontario:[9] 'distinguishing between for-profit and non-profit orientation adds less to understanding how the implications of long-term care restructuring play out ... than focussing on ... key issues that both types of providers face' (Skinner and Rosenberg 2006: 2874).

Finally, profit organisations and non-profit organisations can engage in strategic alliances (Austin 2000). This is analysed in a transaction cost framework by O'Regan and Oster (2000), in two US cases of subcontracting (education and welfare). Galaskiewicz and Sinclair Colman (2006: 180), in a descriptive chapter on collaboration between profit organisations and non-profit organisations in the US, distinguish also three other possible types of collaboration: philanthropic, commercial, and political.

Andreasen (2009: 159-167) provides a more refined taxonomy of cross-sector alliances. The descriptive dimensions of an alliance are the number of partners, the length of commitment, the level(s) of investment, the number of initiatives, the choice between brand-level or company-level collaboration, dedicated resources, the choice between fixed or variable donation amounts, potential grassroots opportunities for company employees and customers. A more fundamental taxonomy can be built on the presence/absence of first order (direct) benefits for the profit organisations and non-profit organisations involved, and the second order (derived or indirect) benefits for both. As to these benefits, he concludes '[t]oday, however, there is only limited evidence' (Andreasen 2009: 155).

Non-profit organisations versus governments

Without any doubt, governments at all levels can be conceived as an answer to the problems caused by the market, except for advocacy and the promotion of ideological, religious or political ideas, at least in democratic and pluralistic states . But governments can also fail in achieving socially optimal governance mechanisms, both at legislative and executive levels (Dollery and Wallis 2003: 27-28).

---

6   Kessler and Mc Clellan 2000, on more than 1.6 million elderly Medicare (US) patients admitted for acute myocardial infarctions in the 1985-1996 period; and Tuckman and Chang (1988), on 115 (1977) and 185 (1992) US nursing homes. For a rather far-fetched model, see Bolton and Mehran (2006: 298-299).

7   401 general acute care hospitals in California (US) in 1990 and 1996.

8   On the presence of 'profitable' services on a sample of more than 46,000 non-rural, non-federal and surgical US hospitals for the 1998-2005 period.

9   72 in-depth interviews held in 2003.

Due to the median voter mechanism, goods or services for which there is a heterogeneous demand are less suited for provision by a government (Ben-Ner and Van Hoomissen 1991: 526; Weisbrod 1988: 25). An assessment of the empirical evidence with respect to the US seems to support this conjecture (Kingma 1997: 140), as well as a direct test with panel data techniques on the size of the non-profit sector in 50 US states (1992-1996), heterogeneity being measured along three dimensions: variation of population age and racial composition, and unemployment (Matsunaga and Yamauchi 2004). In transaction cost terms one could say that provision of a homogeneous good or service by one producer, which is bound to operate with more transparency than private providers (profit or non-profit) due to the presence of an accountability chain (Hansmann 1987: 35), reduces the uncertainty as to the outcome to be expected. Furthermore, governments' income streams are relatively stable and predictable.

The median voter mechanism may also explain why governments are not that good in detecting and satisfying new needs or socially controversial needs. These indeed frequently emerge as 'niche markets', relatively unknown and not always very stable. Current and past examples are: shelters for battered women, HIV/AIDS prevention organisations (Chambré and Fatt 2002; 503), microcredit organisations, adult education organisations, health care centres for prostitutes, or, in general, 'services which react to needs which have formerly been ignored, stigmatised or may not have existed at all' (Badelt 1997: 169).

Other factors may weaken the advantages of government provision of goods and services (Dollery and Wallis 2003: 63 ff): misallocations are possible because of the loose ties between (fiscal) revenues and spending, evaluations are difficult due to complex or vague objectives, and civil servants may pursue their own objectives, to name just a few. They all result in higher production costs and possibly less fair welfare distributions.

When comparing non-profit organisations and public organisations, the point on the importance of exogenous pressures discussed in the previous section can also be raised here: Barbetta *et al.* (2007)[10] study the introduction of a generalised prospective funding mechanism (see Chapter 7) for all hospitals involved, whereas before the introduction public hospitals were funded differently from private non-profit hospitals. Behaviour is reflected through efficiency measures, which differed significantly before the introduction of the prospective payment system, but no longer did so once the system was in place.

Finally, there is also scope for cooperation between government(s) and non-profit organisations, for example in the case of the provision of public goods.[11] Chau and Huysentruyt (2006) present a model in which the private provision of a public good by a non-profit organisation results in a higher welfare level than public provision, in a situation where two organisations are

---

10   Balanced panel of 321 Italian hospitals (1995-2000).
11   Gazley and Brudney (2007: 390-393) present a literature review relating to the cases in which there is no contractual or granting relation between them.

played off against each other in an auction organised by the authorities. An interesting part of their analysis is the integration of the welfare effects at the organisational level caused by the trade-off between ideological purity and payments in this contest. In their empirical work, Gazley and Brudney (2007)[12] observe 'a substantial amount of ... joint activity' (Gazley and Brudney 2007: 397), as about half of both groups of respondents indicated to be involved in non-contractual non-profit/public collaboration, their main motives being the 'desire to secure resources that are more scarce for the respective sector: expertise for government, funding for non-profits.' (*ibid.*: 410).

Notwithstanding the presence of non-contractual relationships, there is also scope for formal relations between governments and non-profit organisations, an example of which is the (partial or complete) outsourcing decision of US local governments with respect to elderly care. Feiock and Jang (2009) provide an original empirical analysis of this 'make-or-(partially)buy' decision, framed in a transaction cost framework including political factors affecting transaction costs (such as political stability and institutional setting), together with the more traditional supply side and heterogeneity factors. Their sample consists of 472 US cities located in metropolitan areas (for 1997), and they indeed find that factors such as the form of government, mayoral turnover, racial segregation, and the presence of non-profit organisations (which all can be translated into transaction cost affecting factors) are related to the decision to outsource elderly services, and, if outsourced, the amount of services outsourced (Feiock and Jang 2009: 677).

Where do we stand?

The previous sections clearly show that, in spite of the substantial intellectual efforts already made by different outstanding scholars, we do not have yet a neat and comprehensive theory explaining the need for non-profit organisations. Salamon and Anheier (1998) reach a comparable conclusion after their, 'preliminary at best' (*ibid.*: 245), empirical work: 'none of the standard theories seem adequate to account for the observed variations in non-profit scale' (*ibid.*: 232).

It is unlikely that such an overarching theory is even conceivable, given the wide diversity of failures and problems non-profit organisations seem to be remedying.

Nevertheless, a number of remarks can be made as to the existing body of theories (Anheier, Ben-Ner 1997: 93; Brody 1996: 464 and 494; Hansmann 1987: 33; Lyons 1993: 306; Steinberg and Gray 1993: 299; Weisbrod 1988: 43):

- most of the theories are conceptual and intuitive. Formal models are very specific, not to say simplistic or sometimes even eccentric in their assumptions;
- most of the theories are useful to explain why the market is not the appropriate institution to govern a given transaction, but remain silent as

---

12   311 public managers in Georgia (US, 2003) and 285 non-profit executives in the same state (2004).

to the choice between public procurement and non-profit organisation's production;

- the predictive power of the different theories is not systematically assessed yet. The available empirical work almost exclusively relates to the US;
- most of the theories discuss the production of goods and services. Less attention is explicitly devoted to advocacy;
- besides market failure and government failure, there might also exist different kinds of non-profit failure, for which Steinberg (2006: 125-127) enumerates a number of possible reasons: insufficient supply, focus on selected segments of potential beneficiaries, 'parentalism' (his politically correct rephrasing of paternalism), amateurism, productive and allocative inefficiency due to the property rights reasoning discussed in Chapter 2. These might lead to all kinds of inefficiencies such as the 'too many actors, too many chiefs, and too much mission' alluded to by Werker and Ahmed (2008: 87-89) when discussing development aid organisations. One has to admit that these or other non-profit failures are seldom considered when justifying the existence of non-profit organisations.

4 Founding a non-profit organisation

Introduction

In Chapter 3 the 'demand' for non-profit organisations was discussed. Here we turn to their 'supply', confining ourselves to organisations founded by entrepreneurs who run them themselves, or, more generally, organisations whose behaviour is under their exclusive control. In Chapter 5 we will go deeper into the economics of multi-layered non-profit organisations, considering boards, managers, and other staff members.

The economic theory of non-profit organisations' supply is even more embryonic than the demand side theory, except for a few contributions from different theoretical points of view, which will be presented in the next sections. Furthermore, and continuing within the same metaphor, theoretical thinking about demand-supply interactions has hardly been conceived yet (Steinberg 2006: 129). An interesting attempt is proposed by Valentinov (2008a), building on Veblen's ideas and a 'division of labour' approach.

Non-profit entrepreneurs

Generally speaking, an entrepreneur will found a non-profit organisation if, in her perception, her utility will increase by doing so, taking alternative ways of action into account (Ben-Ner and Van Hoomissen 1991: 532). If we accept the assumption that there are within the group of potential entrepreneurs individuals whose utility is also affected by the organisational output (Gassler 1997: 268), it is not difficult to understand why non-profit organisations are founded.

A priori, the utility balance can be affected by a number of factors (Ben-Ner and Van Hoomissen 1991: 541). They can be grouped as follows, a plus sign indicating a positive effect on utility, and a minus sign a negative effect:

- market and product characteristics
  - supply of public good or service (–)
  - 'trust' characteristics of good or service (+)
  - expected utility (+)
- personal and social characteristics
  - income (+)
  - education (+)
  - specificity of individual demand (+)
  - social cohesion (+)

Depending on the specific good or service considered, some of these factors may be more or less relevant. Notice also that some of these factors were considered in the previous chapter too: 'consumers may demand services from [non-profit organisations] for the same reasons that make non-profit entrepreneurs form a [non-profit organisation]' (Badelt 1997: 165).

Modelled non-profit entrepreneurship

A model without altruism

A model which does not need to resort to altruistic entrepreneurs to understand the establishment of non-profit organisations was already developed more than 25 years ago by Borjas *et al.* (1983).

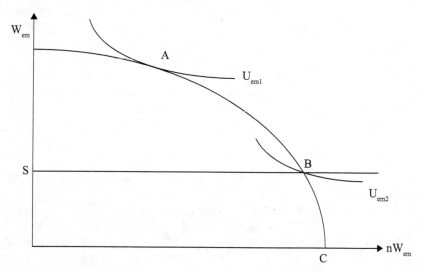

Figure 4.1   Institutional choice by an entrepreneur-manager

Source: based on Borjas *et al.* (1983).

Assume all potential entrepreneur-managers to have identical utility functions U_{em}. Their utility is affected by two factors: monetary wealth (W_{em})

and non-monetary advantages (nW_{em}), which are imperfect substitutes, as illustrated by the transformation curve in Figure 4.1. The location of point C is partly determined by the level of competition the organisation faces, as C moves to the left with increasing competition (Mobley and Bradford 1997: 1130), since competition will make it in general more difficult to survive in the market while visibly 'wasting' too much money.

The entrepreneur-manager reaches her maximal utility (U_{em1}) at point A. Suppose the non-distribution constraint limits the wealth she can obtain to a level S, her maximal utility would be U_{em2} ($<U_{em1}$). As long as S is relatively low, A will not end up between B and C. But combinations of utility function shapes and levels of S are conceivable, though not very probable, in which A is located between B and C on the transformation curve. Then, the entrepreneur-manager is indifferent between a profit organisation and a non-profit organisation.

We can also relax the assumption of each entrepreneur-manager having the same utility function, even if we continue to assume their arguments are still W_{em} and nW_{em}, but allow the weights to differ. Then, for some, the optimum might lie between B and C. They would be indifferent between establishing a profit organisation and a non-profit organisation, and therefore, in a probabilistic perspective, some will found a non-profit organisation. Note that within this line of reasoning, altruism does not have a role to play: 'even if all people were narrow egoists, non-profit firms might still survive in the market place' (Rose-Ackerman 1996: 701).

Another model without altruism is presented by Glaeser and Shleifer (2001). It should be noted, however, that they define a non-profit organisation as an organisation in which the entrepreneur 'is forced to spend [profits] on perquisites' (*ibid.*: 103). Given the confines of the definition given in Chapter 2 we would not call such an organisation a non-profit organisation. In essence, in their model the lower utility of the perquisites to the entrepreneur as compared to the utility of the profits forced to be spent, induces the entrepreneur to increase product or service quality (a source of utility in itself). If this is much appreciated by the consumers they are willing to pay higher prices, even if quality is non-verifiable, as it is precisely the non-profit status (in the Glaeser-Shleifer sense) that guarantees them that higher quality can be expected. Under some circumstances, this status can be optimal from the viewpoint of the entrepreneur. But however interesting this model might be in its own right, it does not really add to our understanding of the founding of non-profit organisations defined in terms of the non-distribution constraint, which is the approach taken in this book.

A model with altruism: the voluntary provision of public goods of some value

Altruism can be defined as the utility a person experiences by somebody else's utility, as rightly or wrongly perceived by the altruist. Therefore, altruists can be expected to take some actions increasing the utility of some group(s) of people (colleagues, workers, club members, women, poor people, art lovers,

...). In order to understand why altruists are not (all) free riders, waiting for other altruists to take the utility enhancing actions, Gassler (1997: 9) assumes that at least some of them must adhere to a Kantian ethic: do to others what you expect them to do for you. Another explanation may be found in religious motives, especially if some utility beyond death is taken into consideration.

In a specific context, Bilodeau and Slivinski (1996,1998) present a model from which it can be inferred that in a society composed of altruistic persons, one of them will eventually set up an organisation providing a public good that is not available yet, at least in case its mere availability is deemed to be of some value. As explained in the previous chapter, if the revenues of public goods cannot be appropriated by their producers, there will be no profit organisation willing to produce the good.

Consider, in a very much simplified version of their model, a society of two non-identical persons, called 1 and 2. They each have a finite time horizon and a utility function U_i (i = 1,2). In each period of time four mutually exclusive states are possible for person i: the public good is not available (state labeled 'n'), the organisation is founded by person i ('f'), the public good is made available through the organisation founded by i ('a'), and the public good is made available through an organisation founded by somebody else ('m'). It is assumed that the act of establishing an organisation comes at a utility cost compared to doing nothing. Furthermore, and here altruism comes in, the public good being available increases i's utility, even after factoring in possible volunteering in the production of the good. This increase is higher if i founded the organisation, because of aspects such as prestige, or the fact of having a decisive influence on the organisation's behaviour. This results in the following ordering of utility levels:

$$U_{i,f} < U_{i,n} < U_{i,m} < U_{i,a}$$

For both persons there is a moment t_i after which founding an organisation will not allow them to compensate the initial utility drop $U_{i,n} - U_{i,f}$ with the discounted utility increases $U_{i,a} - U_{i,n}$. It is even possible that t_i equals zero if the utility investment to found the organisation is relatively high, or if the availability of the public good only marginally increases i's utility, or if the time horizons are too short, or if the discount factor is too high. In such cases there will be no organisation founded, and no public good.

If just one of the two values, say t_1, is strictly positive, than i has no reason not to found a non-profit organisation, as she will increase her utility by doing so, the latest at t_1, but preferably earlier.

Suppose both values are positive, with, without any loss of generality, $t_1 < t_2$. The assumption that persons 1 and 2 are non-identical is reflected by this inequality being strict. At t_2 person 1 might already have founded a non-profit organisation. If not, she will certainly not do so at moment t_2, as this would have a negative utility impact for her. But person 2 now has no rational alternative than to found a non-profit organisation once t_1 has elapsed. This decision will also, as a side effect, increase person 1's utility, but not at person 2's expense.

To sum up, for the provision of a public good to which some value (in a discounted utility sense) is attached by at least somebody in society, a non-profit organisation can be expected to emerge.

Organisational survival

An entrepreneur founding a non-profit organisation is a necessary condition for the establishment of such an organisation, but this is not sufficient for its viability. Anheier and Ben-Ner (1997: 342) list three conditions that should be met:

- there must be a healthy financial basis (see also Chapter 9 on this);
- the organisation must be credible to its stakeholders ('social legitimacy' in an ecological-institutional approach (Baum and Oliver 1996: 1388));
- the organisation should reach such an efficiency level as not to destroy the institutional advantages of being a non-profit organisation.

Furthermore, if the organisation needs not only an entrepreneur, but also (paid or voluntary) collaborators, they must all to be willing to exert the necessary efforts to make the organisation viable. Grimalda and Sacconi (2005: 261-263) provide a simple game-theoretic model to illustrate this.

There are two players in the game: the entrepreneur-manager, and a worker. Each of them can exert two levels of effort: profit maximising efforts (l_{em} and l_w respectively), and a quality enhancing efforts (h_{em} and h_w respectively). Quality improvement implies some kind of volunteering and preferring quality over profit, hence Grimalda and Sacconi's (idiosyncratic) definition of a non-profit organisation as an organisation in which h_{em} and h_w are observed simultaneously (*ibid.*: 262). Since volunteering also implies (partially) working without payment, the worker's real wage under the profit maximising effort (w_l) will be higher than under the quality improving effort ($w_h < w_l$). The additional production cost to improve quality is c_q ($> (w_l - w_h)$) and is incurred whenever the entrepreneur-manager prefers quality over profit, and therefore exerts the effort h_{em}. If both players exert the quality improving effort, societal utility will increase with a value Δu_s as compared to a situation in which both exert the profit maximising effort. If one of the players exerts the quality improving effort, and the other one the profit maximising effort, the effect on societal utility will be $\delta \Delta u_s$ ($\delta < 1$). Π^* is the maximum profit, defined here before wages, and assumed to be large enough to cover for wages and possible quality improving costs. Figure 4.2 displays the payoffs of the game.

49

	h_{em}	l_{em}
h_w	w_h $\Pi^* - w_h - c_q$ Δu_s	w_h $\Pi^* - w_h$ $\delta \Delta u_s$
l_w	w_l $\Pi^* - W_l - c_q$ $\delta \Delta u_s$	w_l $\Pi^* - w_l$ 0

Figure 4.2   Payoff matrix in a profit/non-profit game

Source: based on Grimelda and Sacconi (2005: 262).

The first line in each cell is the worker's wage, the second line the entrepreneur's profit, and the last line societal utility added compared to the profit maximising situation. Not taking into consideration societal effects, the cell (l_w, l_{em}) is the only Nash equilibrium. If both players were altruistic in the sense that Δu_s would affect their utilities, the non-profit solution (h_w, h_{em}) would constitute the only Nash equilibrium, provided that the 'other-regarding attitude towards the beneficiary is sufficiently pronounced among the [worker and the entrepreneur]' (*ibid.*: 263). This is exactly the viability condition described earlier: 'they must all [entrepreneur and collaborators] be willing to exert the necessary efforts'.

5 Governing and staffing a non-profit organisation

Introduction

In Chapter 3 the demand for non-profit organisations was discussed, and in Chapter 4 we turned to their supply, confining ourselves to organisations founded by entrepreneurs who run them themselves, or, more generally, organisations whose behaviour is under their exclusive control. Here, we go deeper into the economics of multi-layered non-profit organisations, considering boards, managers, and other (voluntary and paid) staff members. The basic microeconomic framework for this will be a principal-agent conceptualisation.

The principal-agent framework and non-profit organisations

One of the main assumptions in the previous chapter is that there is no ambiguity as to the objectives of a specific non-profit organisation. These were modelled to be reflected by the organisational utility function U_{npo}, identical to the utility function of the entrepreneur-manager U_{em}. In most real life non-profit organisations, especially the ones that are not very small, the situation is not that simple. Entrepreneurs might be other persons than managers, there can be other stakeholders involved, board members are not identical to one another, possibly (part of the) non-managerial staff is indifferent to the organisation's objectives, volunteers might pursue their own personal objectives, and so on.

A suitable microeconomic framework within which these kinds of situations can be analysed is the *principal-agent* theory. A principal-agent relationship can be defined as 'a contract under which one or more persons (the principal(s)) engage another person (the agent) to perform some service on their behalf which involves delegating some decision making authority to the agent. If both parties to the relationship are utility maximisers there is good reason to believe that the agent will not always act in the best interests of the principal.' (Jensen and Meckling 1976: 308). Part of the principal's problem can be solved by designing appropriate incentive schemes, including some amount of monitoring (at a cost called *monitoring cost*). The agent can commit herself by incurring *bonding costs*, in an attempt to convince the principal she will do her utmost to accommodate his goals. The eventual welfare loss for the principal, as compared to a situation of complete utility alignment, is called the *residual loss*. The sum of monitoring costs, bonding costs, and the residual loss is the *agency cost*.

In general, principal-agent relationships are affected by two categories of problems, each resulting from informational asymmetries between the principal and the agent. Before signing the contract, the potential agent can conceal some relevant but negative information about herself, leading to an *adverse selection* problem. After having signed the contract, the agent can misbehave as long as her behaviour is unobservable (*moral hazard*).

Principal-agent relationships abound within society: between shareholders and managers in profit organisations, managers and subordinates in any kind of hierarchical organisations, patients and physicians, students (and/or their parents) and teachers, firms and their advertising agencies, donors and donation recipients, governments and subsidised organisations, needy people and relief organisations, and elsewhere. Without any doubt various relationships in non-profit organisations can also be analysed within this framework (Brody 1996: 462; Herman and Heimovics 1991; Hewitt and Brown 2000; Miller-Millesen 2003; Steinberg 1990), though this runs counter to the 'stewardship' ideal one might cherish. A closer analysis reveals that this opposition between stewardship theory and principal-agent theory is more virtual than real, as a stewardship relationship can be defined as a principal-agent relationship in which the utility functions of both principal and agent are identical (Caers *et al.* 2006b: 29). In this interpretation a stewardship relationship is a limiting case of the general principal-agent relationship, sometimes, rightly or wrongly, believed to be reality by some principals, as illustrated by J.L. Miller (2002) on a small sample of 12, mostly local, US non-profit organisations from New York and Connecticut: 'the board members generally do not believe that their chief executives will behave opportunistically' (J.L. Miller 2002: 437).

Principals in a non-profit organisation

The board

The board as principal

An almost philosophical question is knowing all the parties whose utilities are affected by a non-profit organisation's activities or the lack thereof. These parties are called organisational *stakeholders*, a stakeholder being '[a]ny person or group that is able to make a claim on an organisation's attention, resources or output, or who may be affected by the organisation' (Lewis 2001: 202). Note that this definition is applicable to all sorts of organisations.

Every stakeholder can act as a principal in a principal-agent theory of non-profit organisations, although board members and (managerial and non-managerial) employees would then have two roles. As there is no reason to expect them all to have identical objectives, and, for that matter, identical perceptions of effectiveness (Herman and Renz 2004: 699), a comprehensive principal-agent approach would imply a multiple principals framework. At the moment of writing, such a non-profit theory has not yet been developed.

In line with mainstream theorising on profit organisations, in non-profit theories the board of directors is acting as if it embodies the organisation's mission, assuming away possible differences in objectives between its principals, even if we only consider the founders of the organisation to be the only principals to reckon with.[1] The board is usually described as a monolithic body, having clear goals and objectives. These goals and objectives can be the result of an averaging process within the board, as described in the next section, but are eventually attributed to the board as a whole.

As in economic theories on profit organisations, non-profit boards are the focal point of analysing 'corporate governance' issues, but unfortunately, compared with the huge amount of theoretical work on profit governance, '[l]ess is known about governance arrangements in non-profit corporations.' (Dyl *et al.* 2000: 335), or 'the economics-based literature has been fairly silent on non-profit governance' (Eldenburg *et al.* 2000: 5). A reason might be the fact that '[n]onprofit organisations have governance problems that resemble the problems in for-profit firms, but are often far more extreme' (Glaeser 2003: 39). By now, the situation has improved. This might be the reason why the above quotation of Eldenburg *et al.* is not found anymore in the published version of their paper (Eldenburg *et al.* 2004).

The impact of the composition of the board on organisational behaviour

One of the first empirical papers delving into the impact of board composition on the behaviour of non-profit organisations is by Dyl *et al.* (2000). Their sample consists of 54 non-profit medical research charities in the US (1991), and focuses on managerial representation on the board, which appears to be positively related to higher executive salaries and more attention to fundraising, but not to management expenses or organisational wealth.

Callen *et al.* (2003) assembled a sample of 108 large New York non-profit organisations in 1995 and 1996. After having described size, gender composition and seniority of board members, they characterise board composition by using five categories of members: staff,[2] major donors, persons with professional skills,[3] well-known individuals, and the inevitable 'others' (Callen *et al.* 2003: 501), and also present information on the existence and composition of all

---

1   One very specific exception (on the effect of the presence of revenue maximising physicians in non-profit hospital boards on quantity-quality decisions) is the paper by Bauer (2009: 471-478).

2   Median value: 2 per cent of board size.

3   The largest group: 37 per cent median value.

kinds of committees. The most frequently observed committees are the finance and nomination committees, in more than 70 per cent of the organisations surveyed. Audit committes are the least frequently observed, in 35 per cent of the cases, though this number amounts to about 80 per cent in the post Sarbanes-Oxley sample (2004) of Vermeer *et al.* (2006),[4] or to about 66 per cent in the sample of Iyer and Watkins[5] (Iyer and Watkins 2008: 261). Further, the composition of the existing committees does not reflect board composition, but seems, logically, adapted to the committees' competences: the median share of professionally skilled members of the audit committees is almost two-thirds of the committees' sizes, whereas this share is lower than one-third for the nomination committees, to give just a few examples (Callen *et al.* 2003: 502). The governance structure in place and the composition of the governance bodies are clearly shown to affect organisational behaviour. More donors on the board go together with less administrative expenses and more core activities, larger boards are positively associated with (relative) fundraising expenses. The effect of the committees as such is not assessed, but donor membership of these committees is. Their presence in finance committees is positively related to the organisation's administrative efficiency (*ibid.*: 515-516).

The link between governance structure and performance is also assessed by Alexander and Lee (2006). They concentrate on the board configuration, looking at the impact of having a 'corporate model' board (Alexander and Lee 2006: 737), characterised by a limited number of paid specialised board members, by including in the board a substantial share of actively participating inside directors, by making managers directly accountable to the board, by setting finite terms of service for the board members, and by a focus on strategic issues. Their data pertain to non-profit hospitals,[6] and reveal only a positive link between the presence of 'corporate model' boards and the level of (adjusted) admissions, and not with efficiency, market share, occupancy, or cash-flow (*ibid.*: 747). De Andrés-Alonso *et al.* (2006) concentrate on the relationship between board characteristics (size, relative number of outsiders, rotation of board members, presence of an executive committee, minimum number of board meetings per year, organisation's founder being a board member) and efficiency.[7] There seems to be no relationship with technical efficiency (measured as the share of administrative costs in total costs), but smaller sizes, larger shares of outsiders, and lower meeting frequencies positively affect what is called allocative efficiency (direct project expenses divided by donations and subsidies) (De Andrés-Alonso *et al.*: 600). These results are not found in a sample of 144 Spanish foundations (2004), where board size and the number of independent board members do not have any effect, contrary to expertise diversity and the number of 'active' board members, which both have a beneficial effect (De Andrés-Alonso *et al.* 2010: 109). Brickley *et al.*

---

4   128 of the largest US non-profit organisations.
5   Larger organisations (36 observations) in a sample of 215 North Carolina (US) non-profit organisations.
6   Three samples of each around 1,000 observations in the period 1985-1993.
7   41 Spanish non-governmental development organisations (1995-2001)

(2010) assess[8] whether CEOs with voting power in the board earn, *ceteris paribus*, higher wages. The answer is 'yes', the difference ranging between 7 per cent and 10 percent, depending on the regression specification (Brickley *et al.* 2010: 200).

Finally, a few studies concentrate on the ultimate owner of the organisation instead of on the board this owner constitutes. Farsi and Filippini (2004), for instance, find no significant efficiency differences between public non-profit organisations and private non-profit organisations,[9] whereas Knox *et al.* (2006) find efficiency differences between private secular non-profit organisations and religious non-profit organisations,[10] the secular ones being more efficient (Knox *et al.* 2006: 658).

Another study with New York data[11] is performed by O'Regan and Oster (2005). Contrary to earlier work, they go into a little bit more detail as to the members' professional skills (financial, other business, education, law, social services) (O'Regan and Oster 2005: 213). Interestingly, the unit of analysis is the board member, and not the board itself or the organisation. The behavioural patterns they discern are complex (*ibid.*: 221). To give one example, they find that the presence of voting executives in the board is inversely correlated with the number of donating board members, but positively with the average amount donated (*ibid.*: 220).

Du Bois *et al.* (2005) try to discover a link between board composition and organisational objectives.[12] Apart from their gender, board members are grouped into members with an educational background, a legal background, a financial background, or a religious background. Using an ordered probit methodology, it is shown that board composition matters in terms of organisational objectives, at least as expressed by the chairperson. To give just one example, the data show that the presence of more men in the board decreases the importance attached to ideology as a key objective of the school.

All in all, the available research is scattered, making detailed generalisations methodologically difficult. Nevertheless, they all point to the conclusion that there is a possibility that the composition of the board, and the governance structure in general, is not neutral as to its effect on the functioning of the organisation.[13] Enacting regulations on board composition, such as for instance on gender representativity, might therefore have unexpected, but not necessarily unwanted or negative, side effects on the organisational objectives effectively pursued.

---

8 308 non-profit hospitals in the US, for the period 1998-2002.
9 Panel data on 36 Swiss nursing homes in the Ticino canton, 1993-2004.
10 About 150 Texan (US) nursing homes in each of the years 1994, 1998, 1999.
11 More than 3,100 board members of 403 non-profit contractors of New York city (data collected in 1999).
12 170 chairpersons of non-profit Flemish (Belgium) primary and secondary schools, data for 2005.
13 See Jackson and Donovan (1999: 18 ff) for an example of a practitioner oriented version of this statement.

Functioning of the board

There is still no real economic theory on the functioning of non-profit boards (Ostrower and Stone 2006: 612), despite the existence of numerous practitioner oriented handbooks on the topic. They mostly depart from 'a "heroic" model of the role of the non-profit board' (Herman and Heimovics 1990: 168), although this might also be considered just to be a normative stance, in line with the recommendations of Fama and Jensen (1983a: 318) for donative non-profit organisations: expropriation of the organisation by managers can be avoided by structurally separating initiative and implementation from fiat and control, the latter two being the competences of the board. Dewaelheyns *et al.* (2009) test this separation directly[14] and observe larger organisations to better implement Fama and Jensen's recommendation (Dewaelheyns *et al.* 2009: 193).

Ostrowski's list (1990: 184) of board tasks is more detailed than Fama and Jensen's one, but fundamentally comparable. The tasks include being the stakeholders' voice and determining and guarding the organisation's objectives (in other words being a good principal), appointing, supporting and evaluating management, long term planning, financial control, activity planning supervision, reputation building, instance of appeal for internal conflicts, assessment of its own functioning. Grouping these tasks results in the three 'roles' proposed by Lee *et al.* (2008: 1227): mission and strategy setting, performance evaluation and oversight, and external relations. Comparing profit hospitals with non-profit hospitals,[15] they observe relatively more non-profit hospitals with 'balanced active boards' (pursuing the three roles in a balanced way) and with 'strategic and external active boards' (*ibid.*: 1233). The board roles described by Ostrower and Stone (2010: 908)[16] can be grouped in the same way. They find 'a great deal of heterogeneity in how actively boards handle … most basic of board roles' (Ostrower and Stone 2010: 907), but with clearly less engagement for external relation roles. Notice that in both studies no relation with organisational performance is investigated.

To assess the non-profit board's functioning, Gill *et al.* (2005) designed and validated[17] what they call the Governance Self-Assessment Checklist, consisting of 144 items grouped into 12 subscales (see Table 5.1).

Finally, as far as prescription is concerned, Preston and Brown (2004: 222) present a literature review from which they derive a list of performance indicators for individual board members: attendance during meetings, input during meetings, organisational knowledge, follow-up of relevant topics, volunteering for operational tasks. The last one does not seem to be essential for a good functioning board member, and even conflicting with the Fama and Jensen recommendation above, possibly affecting independence or psychological distance, but on the other hand it helps the member to get an idea of organisational reality.

---

14   96 Flemish (Belgium) nursing homes (2005), both public and non-profit.
15   1,334 private hospitals in the US (2005).
16   Representative sample of 5,111 US charities (data on 2005).
17   312 respondents, of which 31 executive directors, from 32 Canadian non-profit organisations.

Table 5.1 Subscales of Governance Self-Assessment Checklist for non-profit boards

	Subscale description
1	Board effectiveness quick check (15 items)
2	Board structure (13 items)
3	Board culture (16 items)
4	Mission and planning (13 items)
5	Financial stewardship (10 items)
6	Human resources stewardship (9 items)
7	Performance monitoring (9 items)
8	Community representation (8 items)
9	Risk management (13 items)
10	Board development (10 items)
11	Board management (11 items)
12	Decision-making (17 items)

Source: Gill *et al.* (2005: 277-278, 282).

An early study to assess the non-profit board's functioning is by Middleton (1987), who reviews the (essentially US based) empirical results available at that time. She concludes that 'many board members and managers alike contend that boards often function poorly' (*ibid.*: 141). A more cynical view has been expressed by Brody (1996: 487): '[t]he most important task of the non-profit board is to ensure its own continuation'. But more recent empirical work allows us at least to qualify these observations, though the measurement of organisational performance is not free of validity problems, and most samples are rather small.

Thirty-nine volunteer managed non-profit organisations in a Boston (US) suburb (1992) constituted the sample of Smith and Shen (1996). Reputation, measured by the number of nominations by leaders of other organisations, is seen to be positively affected by the mere presence of a board (*ibid.*: 279). As already mentioned, Callen *et al.* (2003) use efficiency measures to assess organisational performance, and relate them, in a number of cases with statistically significant results, to board characteristics. In the paper by Gill *et al.* (2005) mentioned above, for each organisation in the sample two external observers familiar with the organisation were asked to rate the organisation on ten effectiveness items. Internal effectiveness ratings were also collected. Most of the subscale values of the Governance Self-Assessment Checklist (see Table 5.1) are significantly related to these ratings (*ibid.*: 284). On a sample of 100 non-profit, mostly human service, organisations, Brown (2005) finds significantly positive correlations between organisational performance as perceived by executives and board members, and board performance as perceived by board members and executives respectively (*ibid.*: 331).

Somewhat contrary to the previous results, Herman and Renz (2004)[18] do not find a relationship between the application of 'good' practices by the board and organisational effectiveness as measured by a number of people involved in the organisation.

Other principals

Theoretically, every stakeholder can be considered a principal on its own, instead of the board being seen as a body representing all of them. This has not been incorporated in the extant theoretical literature, except for a casual reference to the organisation's beneficiaries (Williamson 1983: 358) and the donors. As for the latter, Hewitt and Brown (2000: 178) present them as principals, and argue that choosing the non-profit institutional form for a donative organisation constitutes bonding costs on behalf of the entrepreneur, who shows her willingness to pursue the donor's objectives by deliberately forgoing wealth increases out of the organisation's monetary surplus. Therefore, she has no interest in generating such a surplus, as a substitute for more activities in line with the donor's objectives. Brody (1996: 509) does not agree with this reasoning: in her view the non-distribution constraint is not a necessary condition to align the interests of principals and agents. In the paper by De Andrés-Alonso *et al.* (2006: 599-600) mentioned above, the authors establish that the fact of being largely dependent on substantial subsidies granted by a well organised institutional donor suffices to steer organisational behaviour, in that there is a positive impact on both efficiency measures they use. Note that, at least in this case, the institutional donor does not play this role as principal by appointing representatives in the organisations' boards, but through direct links with the organisations themselves.

Turning to organisational staff, the manager, besides her role as an agent of the board (see below), also performs a role as a principal with respect to the subordinate staff. Economic theory on this role in a non-profit context is scanty (Caers *et al.* 2006b: 40-41), although there is some literature on this subject in the context of profit organisations (e.g. Beckman 1988).

Agents in a non-profit organisation

The manager

Managerial utility

Despite their theoretical and practical importance, 'the particular incentives guiding non-profit managers are not well understood by economists' (Thornton 2006: 206). Leaving aside caricatures describing non-profit managers as persons driven only by material self-interest, there is some consensus that they

---

18   Maximally 44 United Way funded organisations in the US (health and welfare organisations, organisations helping developmentally disabled people), data for 1999.

are at least partially motivated or characterised by a form of altruism: 'the people attracted to managerial positions in the non-profit sector are those who care relatively little about financial gain and relatively highly about putting their own ideals into practice' (Rose-Ackerman 1987: 815), or '[t]hick carpets and mahogany furniture for the executives seem to be a popular illustration, at least among those who have not actually seen the administrative offices of many non-profit hospitals.' (Lynk 1995: 444, n19). Therefore we can expect managers in non-profit organisations to earn less than their hypothetically identical counterparts in profit organisations, as the disutility of a lower wage is compensated by the utility effect of managing an organisation that is perceived to do something 'good' for others (a phenomenon called *labour donation*). Note that this conclusion is valid not only when profit managers and non-profit managers are assumed to differ as to the arguments in their utility functions,[19] but even when it is assumed that all managers are identical as far as their utility functions are concerned. Working in a profit organisation, then, does not add utility through altruism, requiring higher wages in order to generate the reservation utility.

The available empirical literature on managerial remunerations seems to confirm this conclusion. In their review, Roomkin and Weisbrod (1999: 754) observe that non-profit managers are paid between 20 per cent and 59 per cent less than comparable colleagues in profit organisations. French data analysed by Narcy (2011: 323)[20] reveal a comparable 20 per cent gap between profit managers and non-profit managers. Preston and Sacks (2010)[21] find a difference of 19 per cent, before controlling for industry. A number of industries have low wages of their own, reducing the difference to a still significant 7 per cent after controlling for industry (Preston and Sacks 2010: 114). Preyra and Pink (2001)[22] find similar differences. They also find managerial wages in non-profit organisations to be more stable than managerial wages in profit organisations, as the latter consist of relatively more performance based bonuses. This last observation is also made by Roomkin and Weisbrod (1999: 772),[23] who show the shares of bonuses to be respectively less than 18 per cent of total wages in non-profit organisations, and more than 40 per cent (excluding options) in profit organisations. Comparable results are presented by Ballou and Weisbrod (2003), who establish[24] that fixed wages for non-profit managers are higher than for profit managers, but that this difference is more than compensated by the amount of bonuses for profit managers. Wage differences therefore can also be understood if non-profit managers are more risk averse than profit managers,

---

19   As in Young (1987: 169) or Buelens *et al.* (1999: 54).
20   12,405 managers surveyed in the INSEE's French Labour Force Survey (1994-2001) in industries with simultaneous presence of profit organisations, non-profit organisations, and public organisations.
21   Almost 3,9 million observations (managers and others) for 2000, based on the 2000 Census (US).
22   Canadian sample of 85 non-profit hospitals and 217 profit organisations for 1995-1996.
23   1992 sample of 1,268 US hospitals,
24   730 US hospitals (data for 1992).

but do not rule out the labour donation idea. In fact, both mechanisms are not mutually exclusive.

A non-US empirical study in this field is Jobome (2006).[25] His results are in line with the US results: managerial remunerations are not statistically affected by the presence of typical monitoring instruments such as audit committees, nomination committees, and remuneration committees. Therefore, non-profit managers seem to be driven by altruism rather than by personal wealth, and 'boards should not necessarily invest in controlling board mechanisms in order to curb agency-assumed CEO pay excesses' (Jobome 2006: 350), though the observed lack of correlation could also be the consequence of 'pervasive managerial entrenchment', a less plausible assumption in the eyes of the author (*ibid.*: 351). However, Jobome's conclusions are not compatible with the results obtained by Cardinaels (2009),[26] who finds that governance characteristics of the supervisory board, consisting of independent members, do affect the top manager's remuneration, after controlling for other relevant economic and organisational factors: a lower share of members with an academic degree and higher board member remunerations have a significantly positive (and substantial) effect (Cardinaels 2009: 69). This result does not preclude the possibility that these wages are still lower than in comparable profit organisations, but at least mitigates the conclusion that the managers involved are fully altruistic.

Finally, Handy and Katz (1998: 252-259) use the observed wage difference in a formal model in which there are altruistic persons and non-altruistic persons applying for a managerial job in a non-profit organisation. Altruism is not observable before contracting. Without doing justice to the complexities of their model (in which also imperfectly testable managerial abilities are included), it can be described by stating that proposing wages that are lower than the reservation wage for non-altruistic applicants generates a self-selecting mechanism in which the non-altruists do not apply: '[l]ower wages will attract managers that are more committed to the cause of the non-profit.' (*ibid.*: 259).

The board as a principal and the manager as its agent

The most frequently studied principal-agent relationship in non-profit organisations is the one between the board, acting as the principal, and the manager, being the agent. Empirical work reviewed by Ostrower and Stone (2006: 617-618) indicates that the balance of power in this relationship is affected by three groups of variables ('b' indicating that higher values of the variable under consideration imply more board influence, and 'm' more managerial power):

- individual variables
  - gender of board members: more female board members seem to make the board less influential;
  - prestige/wealth of board members (see also Chapter 7) (b);

---

25   100 largest charities in terms of their 2000-2001 income in the UK.
26   80 Dutch private non-profit hospitals (data pertaining to 2005).

- — managerial tenure (m);
- — managerial credentials (m).
- • organisational variables
  - — age (m);
  - — size (m);
  - — complexity and degree of bureaucratisation (m).
- • environmental variables
  - — complexity of interorganisational ties, making power more fragmented;
  - — organisational financial dependence on board members (b);
  - — stability (m);
  - — governmental funding (m).

In a seminal theoretical paper on the board-manager relation in non-profit organisations, Steinberg (1986b) proposes an approach allowing the measurement of differences between managerial objectives and board objectives, and therefore assessing the principal-agent gap.

As usual, the method starts from some simplifications. The board is assumed to aim for service maximisation (implying zero profits), whereas the manager, if not constrained, aims for budget maximisation. This last assumption, justified by factors such as prestige, salary, and self-dealing (*ibid.*: 508), could be considered as a caricature, referred to in the previous section, but it is also instrumental in making the reasoning clear. The method consists in estimating a parameter k at the organisational level, the value of which lies between zero and one, zero describing a budget maximising organisation, and one a service maximising organisation: the closer to zero, the more severe the agency problems. This follows from the assumption that the organisational utility function can be written as a function of revenues other than subsidies and funds raised (R), subsidies (S), funds raised (F) as determined by fundraising efforts (f), and administrative costs net of fundraising costs (A), which are assumed to be fixed:

$$U_{npo} = k(R+S+F(f)-f-A) + (1-k)(R+S+F(f)) = R+S+F(f) - k(A+f)$$

Assuming that only the funds raised are affected by the fundraising efforts, maximising the organisational utility with respect to f (assuming the second-order conditions are met) leads to the optimality condition

$$dF/df = k$$

Estimating dF/df, the marginal donative product of fundraising, therefore, is equivalent to estimating k (and the organisational objective function, hence a 'revealed' objective function), and therefore to estimating the severity of the agency problems in the organisation. The interpretation of this condition is straightforward: service maximisers will increase fundraising efforts as long as their revenues net of fundraising costs are positive (k=1), whereas budget maximisers continue to raise funds as long as there is any additional income for the organisation ($k \to 0$).

Taking account of lagged effects of fundraising efforts in this context is easy. Suppose there is just a one-year lagged effect (modelling more years is comparable), and define r to be the discount rate. It is easily shown that the organisational utility at moment t now is

$$U_{npo} = R_t + S_t + F_t(f_t) + (F_{t+1}(f_t)/(1+r)) - k(A_t + f_t)$$

from which the optimality condition

$$\partial F_t/\partial f_t + (\partial F_{t+1}(f_t)/\partial f_t)/(1+r) = k$$

Assuming F(f) is concave, this implies that lagged fundraising effects induce the organisation, given k, to spend more on fundraising than in their absence.

However modelled, k's estimation involves some econometric intricacies we do not deal with here (*ibid.*: 510-515). Steinberg finds[27] welfare organisations, educational organisations, and art organisations to be rather service maximising, and health organisations to be budget maximisers.

Clearly, as acknowledged by Steinberg (*ibid.*: 513-514), his method does not work under a number of circumstances. These include the presence of some forms of financial rationing (for example by imposing a ceiling on the funds that can be collected: $F \leq F_{max}$), a negative effect of fundraising activities on volunteers' motivation (meaning that R and/or A are no longer independent from f), fundraising adding to organisational output (e.g. by informing the public or increasing awareness), all kinds of regulations making unconstrained utility maximisation impossible (e.g. rules on how to spend available funds).

Brooks and Ondrich (2007) extend the Steinberg approach by adding a third arguments to the organisational utility function: quality of service. They model this concept, under a zero profit assumption, to be the ratio of production costs (R+S+F(f,y)–f–A) and the output level (y), leading to the following utility function (Brooks and Ondrich 2007: 132):

$$U_{npo} = k_1(R+S+F(f,y)-f-A) + k_2(R+S+F(f,y)) + (1-k_1-k_2)((R+S+F(f,y)-f-A)/y)$$

with $0 \leq k_1, k_2, k_1+k_2 \leq 1$, and the funds raised also being a function of the output level. For a service maximiser, k_1 equals one and k_2 zero, whereas for a budget maximiser the opposite situation prevails. For a quality maximiser, both parameters are zero. The choice variables being the fundraising efforts (f) and the output level (y), the following testable conditions can be derived (for the proof, see Appendix II; subscripts describe (partial) derivatives):

- for a service maximizer: $F_f = 1$ (as in the Steinberg model) and $(R_y+F_y) = 0$
- for a budget maximizer: $F_f = 0$ (as in the Steinberg model) and $(R_y+F_y) = 0$
- for a quality maximizer: $F_f = 1$ and $(R_y+F_y) - ((R+S+F(f,y)-f-A)/y) = 0$

---

27   2,202 non-profit organisations from four metropolitan areas in the US (1974-1976).

The econometric problems to assess which of these conditions prevails are not discussed here, but they may be found in Brooks and Ondrich (2007: 135-137). In fact, they test[28] each condition separately, arriving at a conclusion in the following form: 'service is not an objective for about 30 per cent of the stations, quality can be ruled out for 49 per cent; and budget is rejected for 69 per cent.' (Brooks and Ondrich 2007: 129).

Contrary to the indirect methods proposed by Steinberg (1986b) or Brooks and Ondrich (2007), Du Bois *et al.* (2006) directly measure potential differences in objectives between non-profit boards and non-profit managers,[29] using a discrete choice methodology combined with a mixed logit estimation (Louviere *et al.*: 2000). They find a stewardship attitude on the part of managers is certainly not present. Ideology appears to be more important for board chairpersons, whereas objectives such as staff satisfaction and pupil satisfaction seem more important for the managers. This implies that at least in their setting agency problems are bound to exist.

Finally, even in cases in which there is no difference in objectives between board and management, differences in ideology, religion, or perceptions on optimal strategies may arise. Theoretically, these are no agency conflicts, but they are clearly practically relevant.

Performance based remuneration

To find incentive mechanisms to discipline managers of profit organisations is, theoretically, not such a difficult task, as is proved by the plentiful academic literature on the matter. For non-profit organisations, this is different (Steinberg 1990): '[t]he core governance problems of [non-profit organisations] arise from their management having generally poor incentives and being shielded from the most potent disciplining devices in for-profit firms, like hostile takeovers, proxy fights, or even independent directors' (Bolton and Mehran 2006: 296). Profits are certainly not an appropriate criterion to use in performance based remuneration schemes, as they divert managerial efforts and attention from the organisational objectives to wealth creation (Preyra and Pink 2001: 511), apart from their potential negative effect on subsidies or donations received.

Finding relevant, objective, measurable and verifiable performance criteria to serve as a basis for the calculation of the managerial remuneration is not easy, but there is some empirical support to argue that this is not impossible, at least to a limited extent. Baber *et al.* (2002) establish[30] a very significantly positive relationship between the relative change in managerial compensation and the relative change in *programme* spending (all expenses minus administrative expenses and fundraising expenses). Despite its significance, the relationship is weak, as a 1 per cent increase in programme spending goes together with a .07 per cent increase in managerial compensation (Baber *et al.* 2002: 687,

---

28   104 non-profit radio stations in the US over the period 1990-1996.

29   503 primary school managers, 187 secondary school managers, and 171 board chairpersons of non-profit schools in Flanders (Belgium; 2005).

30   331 US charities in a four year period at the end of the 1990s.

`n6). Hallock's paper (Hallock 2002) is comparable in its set-up.[31] Performance is measured by a number of variables: size, programme expenses relative to total expenses, and financial revenues. After controlling for industry (being significant on its own) and the organisation (in a fixed effects panel estimation), the only statistically relevant but albeit very small correlation is found between managerial compensation and size (a result also obtained by Jobome in his UK sample described earlier (2006: 347)), which is a very questionable performance variable, as it might also proxy for organisational complexity, in which case it is natural to expect higher managerial wages in larger organisations, irrespective of possible incentive effects. Finally, O'Connell (2005)[32] also cross-sectionally finds a positive relationship between the colleges' reputations (as perceived by administrators of other colleges) and the chief executive's salary.

All in all, these results are not very convincing as to the possibility of finding effective incentive mechanisms as a basis for managerial remuneration in non-profit organisations.[33] The correlations found are implicit at best, and do not allow any conclusion as to causality. Further, the choice of the performance variables, uniform throughout the samples used, need not reflect real organisational objectives. On top of that, when designing incentive based payment systems, there should be no ambiguity with respect to the organisational objectives, as well as to their measurement. If these conditions are not met, performance based remuneration systems will force managers to pursue the objectives implied in this system, departing from the real organisational goals, institutionalising or sometimes even somehow creating principal-agent differences. Therefore, it is no surprise to conclude that optimal remuneration schemes in non-profit organisations are hardly explored,[34] and to observe that bonuses are much smaller relative to the base managerial pay in non-profit organisations when compared to profit organisations.

Finally, one should carefully consider possible derived effects of introducing performance based payment systems in non-profit organisations. A formal presentation can be based on Frey (1997: 429-430). Managerial utility U_m is a function of the certainty equivalent wage w_m and organisational output y (reflecting the altruistic attitude of the manager). Assuming the second-order conditions to be satisfied, the level of output maximising utility can be determined from

$$\partial U_m/\partial y = 0$$

Increasing the incentive sensitivity of the remuneration scheme (IS) affects this optimality condition as follows:

$$(\partial^2 U_m/\partial y^2)(dy/dIS) + (\partial^2 U_m/\partial y \partial w_m)(dw_m/dIS) = 0$$

---

31   9,776 US non-profit organisations (1992-1996).
32   133 non-profit liberal arts colleges in the US (1995-1996).
33   See also the review by Jobome (2006: 335-338).
34   See Brandl and Güttel (2007: 178); Brickley and Van Horn (2002: 228); Preyra and Pink (2001: 511).

Assuming, (mostly) in line with reality and tradition, the manager to be risk averse, the certainty equivalent wage must increase when the wage becomes more variable due to increasing its connection to performance ($dw_m/dIS > 0$). Assuming U_m to be concave in y is also a standard assumption ($\partial^2 U_m/\partial y^2 < 0$). Therefore, the sign of dy/dIS must be the same as that of $\partial^2 U_m/\partial y \partial w$. This can be positive or negative. The interesting case here is the one in which dy/dIS<0, as this would describe a situation in which increasing performance related pressure on managers would result in performance decreasing in terms of output. The reason is that, $\partial^2 U_m/\partial y \partial w$ being negative, the effect of increasing the certainty equivalent wage decreases the marginal utility of output, or, in other words, the impact of altruism on managerial utility. This would be an example of the more general crowding out phenomenon (Frey and Jegen 2001), in which a diminishing altruistic motivation more than compensates the effect on performance through higher wages.[35]

Non-managerial staff

The principal-agent inspired literature on non-managerial staff in non-profit organisations is less developed than the one on managers, and also less conclusive. A reason for this might be that in the empirical research non-managerial staff are seldom approached as a heterogeneous group. A useful distinction could be one between staff performing core tasks (such as nurses and teachers) and staff with more general or secondary tasks (including secretaries and cleaners).

Psychological research[36] shows that, at least for Flemish (Belgium) teachers and nurses, some forms of altruism are relevant to understand the motivations of staff members performing organisational core tasks, as is also the starting point of the theoretical paper on nurses by Heyes (2005). This is less likely in groups of people with more general qualifications, though it certainly cannot be ruled out, as also pointed out by Handy and Katz (1998: 250-251), looking at the available empirical literature.

Generally speaking, most of the available empirical papers, almost all of which are based on US samples, do not find wage differences for non-managerial staff in non-profit organisations.[37] Preston and Sacks (2010)[38] obtain a different result. Before controlling for industry, they find negative differences between 1 and 19 per cent, most of them remaining negative but less so after controlling for industry (Preston and Sacks 2010: 114). Narcy

---

35 See also Chapter 7 (the introductory section on volunteers), and Meier (2007) for a comparable effect on cash donations matched once by a subsidy, which significantly decrease after subsidising has stopped, even compared to the before-subsidy period.

36 De Cooman *et al.*(2007); De Gieter *et al.* (2006); Schepers *et al.* (2005).

37 Erus, Weisbrod (2003), on 242 US hospitals for 1992 and 1997; Leete (2001), on about 4 million US employees, after controlling for industry and job characteristics; Ruhm, Borkoski (2004), on US data for 1994-1998 with the number of observations ranging between 80,000 and 250,000).

38 Almost 3,9 million observations for 2000, based on the 2000 US Census.

(2011: 323)[39] observes a similar difference in France: almost 12 per cent. The subtle econometric research by Mocan and Tekin (2003)[40] leads to an opposite conclusion: 'there exist non-profit mark-ups in both wages and compensation' (Mocan and Tekin 2003: 41), respectively between 6 per cent and 20 per cent, and between 8 per cent and 10 per cent (*ibid.*: 49). According to the authors, the absence of an effective residual control might explain these results (see Chapter 2). This result is comparable to the one obtained by Preston (1988: 348),[41] with comparable differences between 5 per cent and 10 per cent. It is also interesting to note that these differences tend to disappear when the centres experience competition. Another paper showing positive wage differentials for non-profit workers studies Japanese child care employees in both profit and non-profit organisations,[42] the difference being attributed to managerial preferences for higher quality (Noguchi *et al.* 2008: 1091).

Taking a broader view by looking at overall satisfaction with working in a non-profit organisation, Benz (2005) finds,[43] after controlling for wage, working hours, seniority, age, sex and education, a significantly higher satisfaction on the part of people working in non-profit organisations. The univariate results presented by Mosca *et al.* (2007: 75)[44] point in the same direction: being employed in a non-profit organisation makes people more satisfied with their job than being employed in a profit organisation. A comparable study by Borzaga and Tortia (2006)[45] leads to a less clear picture: general satisfaction is higher in religious non-profit organisations compared to profit organisations, but lower in non-religious non-profits (*ibid.*: 233). An opposite ranking is obtained when looking at the specific satisfaction with the wage received (*ibid.*: 234). The results of Lanfranchi and Narcy (2008) on a sample of European employees without higher education[46] suggest that when non-profit employees show higher satisfaction levels than their colleagues in profit organisations, this might be due to the impact of job characteristics more prevalent in non-profit organisations and not considered in previous research, such as autonomy, discretion in the execution of the job, and the fact of not having repetitive tasks (Lanfranchi and Narcy 2008: 353, 360).

---

39   40,073 employes surveyed in the INSEE's French Labour Force Survey (1994-2001) in industries with simultaneous presence of profit organisations, non-profit organisations, and public organisations. Results for 29,296 technicians and supervisors, and 11,234 blue-collar workers are comparable.

40   1,035 child care workers in 398 day care centres in four US states (1993).

41   3,167 observations at the centre level in the US day care industry for federally financed centres (1976-1977).

42   215 observations for 2002.

43   Samples of, respectively, about 9,000 UK observations and 6,000 US observations in the 1990s.

44   2,332 Italian paid workers in 228 personal care facilities (1998).

45   2,066 employees in the Italian social sector (228 organisations, 1999).

46   4,425 employees with a secondary diploma as their highest degree, employed in a service industry, from Denmark, Finland, France, Greece, the Netherlands, Spain, and the United Kingdom (2004). Around 7 per cent was employed by a non-profit organisation (Lanfranchi and Narcy 2008: 335).

Finally, there is also some research on wage differentiation between non-profit organisations. Haider and Schneider (2010) look at the impact of the presence of volunteers on wage levels, and find that 'the expected wage is lower if an organisation has volunteers compared to organisations without volunteers' (Haider and Schneider 2010: 12).[47] Differences range between 7 per cent and 11 per cent (*ibid.*: 14).

As to performance based remunerations schemes, these seem even less conceivable at the non-managerial level than at the managerial level. There might be one exception, namely teacher performance: Lavy (2008)[48] finds a significant but modest improvement of twelfth-grade students' performance in 17 Israeli schools[49] after having unconditionally increased with 50 per cent the headmasters' wages, and Maralidharan and Sundararaman (2009), in their very elaborated experiment in 300 Indian primary schools in the Andra-Pradesh state (2006-2008), find a substantial increase in pupil performance after having introduced a (modest) bonus system, not only on the bonus related tests, but also on other educational outcomes.

Selecting the agent

Given the fact that agency problems can also be present in non-profit organisations, appropriately selecting agents is one of the ways by which principals might try to reduce these problems, together with designing incentive based remuneration systems, if possible. Surprisingly, only the latter have been extensively studied in the general principal-agent literature, despite the fact that there is no reason to assume that the former are less effective in making the organisation to aim for the principal's objectives. One notable exception is the paper by Besley and Ghatak (2005), in which the selection of agents in non-profit organisations is dealt with. What follows is based on their model.

Consider the risk-neutral principal of a non-profit organisation striving for an organisational output π, which includes non-monetary components (transformed to monetary values). Output depends on the risk-neutral agent's unobservable and therefore uncontractable effort e, scaled in such a way that it also reflects the probability of success. The agent's disutility of effort is $-e^2/2$. Her minimal subsistence wage is w_{min}, and her reservation utility U_{min}. In case of failure, both the principal's and the agent's utilities are just zero. It is assumed that all the variables involved take such values that the optimality conditions for interior solutions are met (*ibid.*: 619, 620).

There are three types of potential agents (indexed i = 0, 1, 2), the types being observable by the principal. Type zero is an agent with only monetary objectives, type one has non-monetary objectives different from the principal's objectives, and type two has objectives identical to the principal's objectives. On top of the utility induced by her wage, consisting of a fixed part w_i and a

---

47   39,613 employees working in 421 Austrian non-profit organisations (2005).
48   See also Lavy (2010) for qualitatively comparable results.
49   Around 1,620 pupils in the period 1995-1998.

bonus b_i ($< \pi$) for success, the agent experiences also a non-pecuniary benefit θ_i, which can be interpreted as her motivation (*ibid.*: 618-619). As it can be assumed that an agent will be more motivated the more her objectives resemble the principal's objectives, we can depart from the following ordering of θ_is:

$$\theta_2 > \theta_1 > \theta_0 = 0$$

The maximisation problem for the principal then is:

$$\max_{i, w_i, b_i} (\pi - b_i)e_i - w_i$$

subject to

$$w_i \geq w_{min} \qquad \text{(subsistence constraint)}$$
$$U_i = e_i(b_i + \theta_i) + w_i - e_i^2/2 \geq U_{min} \qquad \text{(participation constraint)}$$

The agent's utility maximising effort (for i = 0,1,2) is easily seen to be $e_i = b_i + \theta_i$. In Appendix III (part 1) it is proved that $w_i = w_{min}$ for all i. For a given agent type i, it is now easily seen that the principal's utility is maximised when $b_i = (\pi - \theta_i)/2$ (Appendix III, part 2): higher motivation therefore goes together with smaller bonuses (*ibid.*: 621, Corollary 3), a conclusion in line with the empirical results reviewed in the preceding sections. Using this expression learns that e_i is equal to $(\pi + \theta_i)/2$: higher motivation leads to higher efforts by the agent (*ibid.*: 621, Corollary 2).

The only question to be resolved, in fact the main question, is to know which type of agent will be selected by the principal. As the principal's utility function can be written as (Appendix III, part 3)

$$((\pi + \theta_i)^2/4) - w_{min}$$

it is clear that the agent with the highest motivation is to be selected: the applicant pursuing the same objectives as the principal.

A comparable three categories typology is used in the analytical paper by Caers *et al.* (2005b). They extend the analysis by also taking characteristics of a potential client into consideration,[50] when also considering three observable types of agents with utility functions U_i: selfish agents (comparable to the case i = 0 of Besley and Ghatak (2005), but with a more explicit utility function with income, reputation and effort as arguments), 'external stewardship agents', looking predominantly at the potential client's interests (i = 1), and 'internal stewardship agents', fully aligned with the organisational goals (i = 2). Organisational goals are modelled as successfully serving the right type of clients. By construction, selecting internal stewardship agents is optimal

---

50   Is it a client covered by the organisational objectives, how is this perceived by society, and how difficult is the client's case.

from the point of view of the principal.[51] The interesting result, however, is that, under some realistic combinations of agent reputations and client's case difficulty levels, external stewardship agents or even selfish agents can contribute to the achievement of the organisational goals. This implies that non-profit organisations confronted with a shortfall in supply of internal stewardship agents can recruit in a number of situations other types of agents without jeopardising organisational performance.

Resorting to numeric simulation techniques because of analytical intractability, this line of analysis is broadened in different directions (Caers *et al.* 2005a, 2006a). Agent types are combined by considering utility functions of the form

$$U_a = \beta_0 U_0 + \beta_1 U_1 + \beta_2 U_2$$

with $\Sigma \beta_i = 1$, more potential clients are introduced, and finally situations with a board selecting a manager, a manager selecting one up to three employees with different levels of time pressure, and 12 clients are numerically analysed. Also here the results show that under realistic circumstances less than fully committed managers and employees may make their utility maximising decisions in such a way that they do not materially affect organisational performance.

What about volunteers?

Although the academic economic and managerial literatures on volunteers are extensive, it is surprising to observe that they seldom discuss topics dealing with the functioning of non-profit organisations within agency or governance frameworks (Sampson 2006: 364). The mere existence of these literatures makes it improbable that the organisational impact of volunteers would be comparable to the impact of professionals, as also implied by Liao-Troth and Dunn (1999: 346, 347). Furthermore, in a principal-agent reasoning it seems unwarranted not to make a distinction between voluntary principals and voluntary agents. An empirical justification for this distinction is found in Hustinx (2005: 635-640), who discerns in her sample of volunteers working for the Flemish Red Cross (Belgium) five styles of volunteering, one of which to a great extent corresponds to the group of voluntary board members, also called 'a unique group of volunteers' by Preston and Brown (2004: 222), who further observe that boards in numerous non-profit organisations consist almost exclusively of volunteers (*ibid.*: 221). In the same vein, Handy (1995) explicitly models the decision of a volunteer to join a board, taking into consideration wealth and reputation effects (see Chapter 7 for more details). But all these scholarly efforts do not preclude the fact that 'almost no research has been conducted on how or the extent to which board volunteering affects the achievements of the organisation' (Herman 2005: 78). Clearly, there is on this topic much scope for further pathbreaking research.

---

51   Which is in fact the conclusion reached by Besley and Ghatak (2005).

6 Organisational strategy and behaviour of non-profit organisations

Introduction

After having discussed the role of day-to-day strategic planning in non-profit organisations, this chapter introduces some economic models describing non-profit strategy. Most of them are comparative: differences in strategic reactions to exogenous shocks between non-profit organisations on the one hand, and profit organisations (or governmental bodies) on the other hand are analysed. A few focus on the outcomes of competitive processes involving non-profit organisations and profit organisations.

Strategic planning in non-profit organisations

The importance of strategic planning for non-profit organisations can hardly been overestimated, as is also the case for other organisations. Conceptually, there is no real difference between strategic planning for non-profit organisations and other organisations, as it is the outcome of an organisational reflection on how to reach organisational objectives, however defined.[1] The difference lies in the objectives themselves (see Chapter 2), and in the presence of specific constraints and circumstances, such as the diversity of stakeholders and financial sources, the importance of non-market influences (Middleton and Greer 1996: 634), or the non-distribution constraint. K.D. Miller (2002) even shows that the mainstream techniques of strategic planning can be applied to religious organisations, which literally produce *credence goods*, defined as goods or services whose quality cannot be ascertained before or during their consumption, unless perhaps in another life. A comparable idea, confined to the realm of strategic marketing of religious organisations, is implicit in the research overview by Mottner (2008).

---

1   For another view, see Moore (2000: 184).

A good example of a planning system for non-profit organisations is proposed by Bryson (1991: 48):[2]

- identify the organisation's scope;
- determine the objectives;
- perform a SWOT analysis;
- identify the relevant strategic issues;
- choose an appropriate strategy or appropriate strategies;
- implement this strategy or these strategies.

Obviously, there is no fundamental difference between this system and the ones found in management textbooks for profit organisations.

Looking at 17 empirical papers published between 1977 and 1992, Middleton and Greer (1996) try to establish a global picture of planning in donative non-profit organisations. Their first observation is that 'formal planning was not widely used' (Middleton and Greer 1996: 636). Four factors seem to induce formal planning (*ibid.*: 636-640): requirements by donors, organisational difficulties or challenges (such as decreasing membership, managers leaving the organisation, changing target groups, changing priorities of main funders), managerial commitment to planning, and size, the larger organisations being more inclined to have a formal planning system than the smaller ones. Courtney (2002: 115-118) refers to a survey study by an accounting firm (Clark Whitehill) on larger UK charities,[3] of which 82 per cent reported to apply some form of strategic planning. Given the fact that only larger organisations were surveyed, this result does not contradict Middleton and Greer's conclusions. Finally, Hwang and Powell (2009: 279) observe that almost half of the 190 organisations in their random sample of San Francisco Bay Area (US) non-profit organisations had strategic planning procedures.

The review by Stone *et al.* (1999) goes beyond the descriptive, as it attempts, looking at 65 empirical research papers published between 1977 and 1997, to establish links between strategic management activities (strategy formulation, strategy content, and implementation) and organisational performance. The findings at the descriptive level are in line with the ones discussed in the previous paragraph. As far as the impact on performance is concerned, the research reviewed has remained silent (as it still is), one of the reasons probably being the difficulty of unequivocally measuring organisational performance (Stone *et al.* 1999: 417). In consequence, none of the studies reviewed includes specific measures of performance (*ibid.*: 407).

Despite the number of practitioner oriented publications in the field of strategic planning for non-profit organisations, and the empirical work available on the matter, there appears to be no generally accepted theoretical framework within which strategic behaviour of non-profit organisations can be analysed: '[t]here is no accepted theory of [non-profit] behaviour, and little of the empirical work is connected to ... existing theories' (Malani *et al.* 2003: 181-182). These existing theories, some of which ignore the principal-agent situations referred

---

2   See also Anheier (2005: 261).
3   Most of them having annual sales exceeding GBP 1 million.

to in Chapter 5, are grouped by Malani *et al.* (2003) into three clusters of models: altruism models,[4] physician cooperative models,[5] and models departing from non-contractible quality (Glaeser and Shleifer 2001). Confronting these models with the available empirical evidence, they conclude that 'the physician cooperative model is not empirically relevant' (*ibid.*: 211). Furthermore, the strategic implications of these models are not their core points of interest.

Most of the more elaborate available theoretical work has a comparative nature, as it compares in very specific circumstances organisational behaviour of non-profit organisations with that of profit organisations. Some examples of this will be presented in later sections. Managerial economic theory comparing the behaviour of non-profit organisations with that of public authorities is not available yet.

Strategic choices

Economics and non-profit organisations' strategies

Theorising on organisational strategy still is quasi-monopolised by a profit organisation's point of view, which gave rise to well known strategies such as the *generic strategies* advanced by Porter (1980),[6] or diversification strategies described by, among others, Ansoff (1965). As long as it is kept in mind that non-profit objectives differ from profit organisations' objectives, these contributions are also valuable for boards and managers of non-profit organisations, as illustrated by Tuckman (1998a: 179-183), who applies the Porter framework of the 'five competitive forces' (Porter 1980) to non-profit organisations competing with each other.

It is fair to say that the theories mentioned above do not stem from the field of economics, which entered the domain of strategic management once agency problems within firms were studied. Organisational behaviour is then explained either as fully determined by management (the 'managerial theories' of the firm), or as the outcome of the interplay between organisational principals and agents. An early example is the growth maximisation theory to which the name of Baumol (1959) is inextricably connected. Whereas a profit organisation pursuing growth is, except in some rare circumstances, deviating from its main objective (profit maximisation), a non-profit organisation with the same goal need not suffer from this problem, as deploying as much activities as possible might be a perfectly acceptable objective. In that context, Galaskiewicz *et al.* (2006) empirically assess the impact of networking on organisational growth.[7] Even after controlling for status differences, donative non-profit organisations involved in social networks showed higher growth

---

4   Going back to Newhouse (1970), in which organisational utility is determined by both
     output quantity and output quality. See Chapter 2.
5   Originating in Pauly and Redisch (1973), where the absence of residual claimants transfers
     control over resources to the physicians in a non-profit hospital.
6   Cost leadership, differentiation, focus.
7   156 public charities located in Minneapolis-St Paul (US; 1980-1994 data).

rates than donative organisations not involved in such networks, whereas the reverse was observed for commercial non-profit organisations (Galaskiewicz *et al.* 2006: 368), suggesting for the latter that the cost of establishing such a network is not compensated by activity growth.

Technically, growth is also constrained by financial factors. These are elucidated in the next section, based on Jegers (2003).

Sustainable growth for non-profit organisations

As infinitely growing is impossible, growth rates for non-profit organisations are constrained in different ways, as for all kinds of organisations. Here we look at financial constraints, allowing for a maximal growth rate which is called the 'sustainable growth rate' (SGR) of the organisation. As proved in Appendix IV, this growth rate, defined as the relative change in output between years one and zero $((y_1-y_0)/y_0)$ will be affected by the change in the amount of debt, the change in profits, and the change in efficiency in the following way:

$$SGR = \frac{(1+d_1)\alpha'}{(1+d_0)(1-(1+d_1)m)} - 1$$

with d_t being the organisation's capital structure expressed as the ratio of debt and equity at the end of year t (D_t/Eq_t), m being the return on assets for year 1 (including all gifts, donations and subsidies), and α' reflecting the change in efficiency during year 1, expressed as an index: output per unit of total assets for year 1 divided by the same ratio for year zero $(\alpha_1/\alpha_0 = (y_1/TA_1)/(y_0/TA_0))$. The formula for the SGR, which is nothing more than a technical equation showing the financial limits of organisational growth, implies that higher growth rates can be achieved with higher debt rates (higher values of d_1), higher profit rates (m), and more pronounced efficiency gains (α'), as can be intuitively expected. The intuition behind the effect of increasing debt is that additional debt increases the impact of each currency unit of profits on total assets, resulting in a larger asset base for organisational activities.

Special cases allow straightforward simplifications of the above formula: no changes in capital structure and efficiency ($d_0=d_1$ and $\alpha'=1$), no changes in capital structure and no profits ($d_0=d_1$ and m=0), no profits and no efficiency gains (m=0 and $\alpha'=1$).

Location

In spacious countries the location of a non-profit organisation is an important strategic decision, possibly constraining further strategic choices, as illustrated by Castaneda and Falaschetti (2008), who empirically establish that, once controlled for location, a hospital's institutional character (profit, non-profit, public) does not affect its scope of activities.[8]

---

8   More than 4 million procedures grouped in 16 main procedure categories, in 920 hospitals in 22 US states, for 1997 (Castaneda and Falaschetti 2008: 131-132).

A more direct test is provided by Harrison (2008).[9] She simultaneously considers the impact of taxes and agglomeration effects (other non-profit organisations already present in the same industry, and in all other industries) on location decisions, and finds higher individual tax rates to be positively related to the location of new organisations, probably through a 'price of donations' mechanism (see Chapter 7). There is also a concave relationship of location choice with within-industry agglomeration, implying that the presence of comparable non-profit organisations attracts new entrants, but at a diminishing rate.

Comparing strategic behaviour of non-profit organisations and profit organisations: some examples

The effect of an exogenous demand change on organisational charity

The model by Banks *et al.* (1997) relates to a mixed hospital market with profit hospitals and non-profit hospitals. They compare the impact of an exogenous demand change, possibly detected by a SWOT analysis, on the supply of uncompensated care by profit hospitals with that supply by non-profit hospitals. As will be shown below, supply of uncompensated care by profit hospitals is predicted to decrease, whereas supply of uncompensated care by non-profit hospitals is expected to increase.

Assume the organisational utility of the non-profit hospital U_{np} is affected only by the amount of uncompensated care (N), and that uncompensated care will be provided as long as the hospital is not rendered loss-making. Further, demand for uncompensated care is higher than the amount that can be supplied. Therefore, the hospital's optimisation problem can be written as:

$$\max_{y,N} U_{np} = U_{np}(N)$$

$$\text{subject to } \Pi = 0 = P(y;d).y - V(y,N) - F_x$$

where y is the amount of compensated care, d is a demand parameter, $P(y;d)$ is the inverse demand function, and F_x and $V(y,N)$ are the fixed and total variable production costs respectively. Writing $V(y,N)$ instead of $V(y+N)$ allows for the possibility that compensated care and uncompensated care are delivered in different ways. In Appendix V (part 1) it is shown that an increase in demand (through an increase in the value of the parameter d), will result in an increase of the amount of uncompensated care provided by the non-profit hospital, whereas, under fairly general conditions, a profit hospital would behave in the opposite way, even when some tax or fine is to be paid if not enough uncompensated care is provided (Appendix V, part 2). This difference has, of course, an economic interpretation: as non-profit hospitals want to provide as

---

9   16,541 organisations in 48 states (US), for 1997 and 2002.

much as possible uncompensated care in this model, they will take advantage of demand increases in order to generate more funds enabling them to extend their supply of uncompensated care. Conversely, with increasing demand the marginal cost of uncompensated care to a profit hospital will increase, resulting in a lower value of N at the newly established optimum.[10]

Interesting empirical results on exogenous demand shocks in mixed hospital industries are produced by Hansmann *et al.* (2003). They assess the effect of decreases in demand on capacity decisions[11] and find that religious non-profit hospitals will be more reluctant in reducing their number of beds as compared to profit hospitals and public hospitals.

Non-profit organisations involved in mergers

As mergers and acquisitions automatically increase the market shares of the organisations involved, and hence their market power, one can wonder whether merging non-profit organisations will use this increased power in another way than profit organisations. Lynk (1995) reviews the empirical literature up to 1995, mostly relating to the US, and concludes that profit hospitals apply higher prices than their non-profit counterparts after a merger. However, in their more recent literature review on the matter, Zaleski and Esposito (2007: 317-320) reach the conclusion that 'the current supply of research has not provided a definitive answer' (Zaleski and Esposito 2007: 317).

Lynk's empirical work (1995)[12] shows that profit hospitals with market power indeed apply higher prices compared to non-profit hospitals, contrary to the result of the case study by Vita and Sacher (2001)[13] in which, after a number of mergers, two non-profit hospitals were left, applying higher prices than justified by quality considerations. Their conclusion is that competition policy and regulation should apply to both profit organisations and non-profit organisations, as both can be tempted to misuse market power, an insight also seemingly reached by Philipson and Posner (2006) after a microeconomic analysis. Unfortunately, their definition of non-profit organisations does not include the non-distribution constraint, as the consumption of the entrepreneur-manager is modelled to be the sum of income not generated by the organisation and organisational profits (Philipson and Posner: 6), making their use of the term 'not-for-profit' confusing, if not misleading.[14]

Zaleski and Esposito (2007: 320) argue that the use of prices when assessing abuse of market power in the hospital industry may not be a good idea, as they are subject to all kinds of regulations. They propose output and its relations to capacity to be a better indicator, assuming that abuse of market power translates

---

10   Other comparative static results on charity care of non-profit hospitals are provided by Frank and Salkever (1991: 431-434), who compare two kinds of non-profit hospitals.
11   About 2,500 US hospitals between 1985 and 1994.
12   2,981 discharges in 303 Californian hospitals (US; 1989).
13   City of Santa Cruz (US).
14   The paper by Prüfer (2010) on mergers between non-profit organisations follows the same logic.

into investments in excess capacity, meant to deter potential entrants. Their (cross-sectional) empirical results[15] show that non-profit hospitals 'ignore market power altogether when determining capacity utilisation' (Zaleski and Esposito 2007: 322), though longer-term patients seem to be admitted (*ibid.*: 324), whereas other hospitals take advantage of possible economies of scale when in a situation of market power.

Note that concluding that merging non-profit organisations is not harmful is not meant to imply that competition between non-profit organisations cannot be beneficial. In the case of output maximising organisations, convex cost functions C(y), and a zero profit constraint, this can easily be shown. Assume a linear inverse demand function for the output of a non-profit organisation:

$$P = \alpha - \beta y$$

Organisations maximise output subject to

$$\Pi = 0 = Py - C(y)$$

Suppose there is just one supplier. Then the optimal output will meet

$$y^* = (\alpha - P^*)/\beta = (\alpha - C(y^*)/y^*)/\beta \tag{6.1}$$

which has a unique solution due to the convexity of C(y).

If there are two identical suppliers (generalising to more than two suppliers is straightforward) both have to satisfy (i = 1,2):

$$\Pi_i = 0 = Py_i - C(y_i)$$

from which

$$P(y_1 + y_2) = C(y_1) + C(y_2) \text{ or } P = (C(y_1) + C(y_2))/(y_1 + y_2).$$

Market output still has to meet

$$(y_1^* + y_2^*) = (\alpha - P^*)/\beta = (\alpha - ((C(y_1^*) + C(y_2^*))/(y_1^* + y_2^*)))/\beta \tag{6.2}$$

It is impossible that the market equilibrium would be at the same level as in the situation with one supplier, as the left-hand side of equation (6.1) would then be equal to the left-hand side of equation (6.2), whereas the convexity of C(y) makes the right-hand side of (6.2) larger than the right-hand side of (6.1). Increasing the total market output is the only way to meet condition (6.2). An increase in the number of output maximising competitors, and therefore an increase in competition, increases the performance of the industry, measured in terms of output. Note that in this specific case no abuse of a dominant position in the absence of competition is assumed.

---

15   869 US hospitals for the period October 1996 to September 1997.

Competition between non-profit organisations and profit organisations

The crux of strategic behaviour being the pursuit of objectives, competitive strategies of profit organisations and non-profit organisations in the same industry must differ. Frequently competition by non-profit organisations is considered to be unfair by their profit competitors, as the former enjoy all kinds of advantages, such as tax exemptions, lowering their production costs. Liu and Weinberg (2004) present a model from which it follows that the main impact on the profit organisations' profits does not stem from competitive advantages enjoyed by their non-profit competitors, but from the mere fact that the latter have other objectives which affect market outcomes, even if there would be no privilege whatsoever granted to them. A simplified version of their (arithmetically very complex) model will be presented here.

The model describes a price competition (Bertrand-Nash) game in a duopoly, one player being a profit organisation ($i = p$), the other a non-profit organisation maximising its output under a zero profit constraint ($i = np$). The outputs are not identical, but partly substitutable, θ describing the degree of substitutability. Demand is

$$q_i = \tfrac{1}{2}\,(1 - P_i + \theta P_j)\ (i \neq j)$$

The intercept with the P_i-axis (where $q_i = 0$) being 1 for $\theta=0$ or $P_j=0$ implies $P_i < 1$. Further, it is reasonable to assume that the effect of j's price on the demand for i will be lower than that of i's price ($0 \leq \theta < 1$). Average costs (c) equal marginal costs, implying no fixed costs and total variable costs being linear in output. We allow the costs of the profit organisation to differ from the costs of the non-profit organisation, incorporating the possibility of cost advantages enjoyed by non-profit organisations, e.g. because they are tax exempt or subsidised: $0 < c_{np} \leq c_p < 1$. The last inequality logically follows from $P_i < 1$.

The profit organisation's profit is

$$\Pi_p = \tfrac{1}{2}\,(P_p - c_p)(1 - P_p + \theta P_{np})$$

from which the optimal price, taking P_{np}^* as given (Appendix VI, part 1)

$$P_p^* = \tfrac{1}{2}\,(1 + \theta P_{np}^* + c_p)$$

Given the zero profit constraint, the non-profit organisation's output maximising price P_{np}^* equals c_{np} (Appendix VI, part 2), which is also intuitively evident. Therefore

$$P_p^* = \tfrac{1}{2}\,(1 + \theta c_{np} + c_p)$$

which is greater than P_{np}^* as $(1 + c_p) > 2P_{np}^* (= 2c_{np})$, even in the case there would be no cost advantage to the non-profit organisation ($c_{np} = c_p$). It is also easy to see that the profit organisation's optimal price is lower when in a duopoly with a non-profit organisation, as compared to the case of a profit organisation being its competitor. This applies also when there is no cost difference between the two kinds of organisations (Appendix VI, part 3). As a result, consumer welfare is higher.

The final assessment is in terms of profit: does competition by non-profit organisations, be it unfair or not, affect the profit level obtained by the profit organisation in the market? In Appendix VI (part 4), it is shown that the main (negative) effect on the profit organisation's profit clearly does not stem from possible cost differences induced by advantages granted to non-profit organisations, but from the fact that the latter pursue other pricing strategies, in accordance with their objectives. Their profit competitors then have to price differently than when competing with profit organisations: the mere presence of non-profit organisations in the market affects the incumbent profit organisation's strategy, leading to lower profit levels than the ones that could be obtained when competing with other profit organisations. A comparable result, but concentrating on welfare, is obtained by Hirth (1999), who develops a model of competition, under asymmetric information between organisation and consumer, between profit organisations, 'true' non-profit organisations, and non-profits 'in disguise'.

These conclusions are seemingly contradictory to the one analytically reached by Lakdawalla and Philipson (2006), who find that in mixed industries 'marginal industry behaviour is identical to that of a for-profit industry' (Lakdawalla and Philipson 2006: 1681). As they use the same definition of a non-profit organisation as Philipson and Posner (2006) (see the previous section), however, their conclusion is not applicable to non-profit organisations as they are defined in the present text. The same observation applies to the analytical work by David (2009) on size convergence between profit organisations and non-profit organisations.

Comparing strategic behaviour of non-profit organisations and public providers

Although there is some managerial economic work on strategic differences between non-profit organisations and profit organisations, this is not at all the case when comparing non-profit organisations with governmental providers of goods and services: 'theory ... is not strong enough to specify a confident prediction of whether governmental and non-profit providers will or will not behave differently under each of a variety of conditions' (Kapur, Weisbrod 2000: 278). Therefore, empirical work in this field floats in a paradigmatic vacuum. Kapur and Weisbrod (2000) introduce a few building blocks for a comprehensive theory. They look at two dimensions of organisational behaviour: accessibility and service quality.[16] For both industries, public organisations were observed to attach more importance to accessibility than

---

16   Nursing homes and psychiatric facilities (US) for 1976 (109 and 279 observations respectively) and 1987 (99 and 221 observations respectively).

their non-profit counterparts, and less importance to service quality. In a more recent study[17] Amirkhanyan *et al.* (2008: 345) reach a different conclusion as to quality of care, as they do not observe a significant difference (and also notice that quality of care is significantly lower in profit organisations).

---

17   14,423 US nursing homes (2000-2003).

7 Marketing in non-profit organisations

Introduction

At a conceptual level, marketing management for non-profit organisations is not different from marketing management for profit organisations, as both are geared to satisfy some target groups' needs, albeit pursuing different goals (Shapiro 1973: 262), the traditional 'four Ps' (product, price, place, promotion) being equally important for both kinds of organisations. This might be a reason why there is almost no literature on the managerial economics of non-profit organisation marketing, contrary to the abundance of practitioner oriented marketing management handbooks,[1] or the marketing research based literature.[2] Exceptions in this theoretical vacuum consist of work on specific non-profit related aspects such as volunteering, fundraising (donations, gifts, subsidies), and the development of activities aimed at generating profits. These aspects will be taken up in the present chapter.

Marketing management

A hostile attitude towards marketing techniques characterised the majority of non-profit organisations for decades, with marketing being perceived as some capitalistic witchcraft aimed at making capitalists richer. Nowadays a more realistic approach is observed and '[f]or profit marketing and management concepts have ... become acceptable concepts in the non-profit sector realm.' (Shoham *et al.* 2006: 454), though 'the impact of [an organisational marketing orientation] on performance of not-for-profit organisations has been underresearched and has not been reviewed or meta-analysed to this date' (*ibid.*: 456). Shoham *et al.* (2006) then perform a meta-analysis themselves, for which they could find only 11 usable research papers, on 1,589 non-profit organisations from different industries and from six developed countries located in three different continents

---

1   An example of which is the excellent research-based text by Sargeant (2005).
2   Nicely reviewed in the volume edited by Sargeant and Wymer (2008).

(*ibid.*: 461). Their conclusion is that the presence of a marketing orientation indeed positively affects organisational performance, even significantly more than for profit organisations (*ibid.*: 464). A possible explanation for this difference could be the fact that the levels of marketing orientation in profit organisations are more or less comparable, mitigating differentiating effects on performance, whereas non-profit organisations embracing a full marketing approach (still) enjoy some kind of first mover advantage. The fact that the marketing orientation-performance link is significantly weaker in the US than in the other countries covered (*ibid.*: 466) can be understood by a comparable reasoning. Also relevant in this context are the results obtained by Ritchie and Eastwood (2006) who found[3] that 'executives with marketing backgrounds had the greatest impact on financial performance' (*ibid.*: 76), financial performance being measured in terms of fundraising performance.

Pricing

In the previous chapter pricing was presented as a component of strategic management and organisational behaviour, but as such it pertains to the domain of strategic marketing, as long as the pricing decision is taken within the organisation.[4] As already mentioned, there are few economic analyses of pricing decisions of non-profit organisations, and most of them are performed in a comparative context, as the examples in the previous chapter show.

In this chapter, Niskanen's (1971: Chapter 9) treatment of a monopolistic non-profit organisation is discussed, in a market with the following inverse demand function:

$$P = \alpha - \beta y$$

with positive parameters and $0 \leq y \leq \alpha/\beta$ to ensure positive prices. Revenues equal

$$R = Py = \alpha y - \beta y^2$$

and production costs, again with positive parameters

$$C = \chi y + \delta y^2$$

To be viable, the organisation's revenues should at least cover the costs ($R \geq C$). As only situations in which $\alpha > \chi$ are economically relevant, this implies

$$y \leq (\alpha - \chi)/(\beta + \delta) \ (< \alpha/\beta)$$

---

3   144 executive directors of US non-profit university and college foundations.
4   See Prieto-Rodríguez and Fernández-Blanco (2006) for an agency model in which the subsidising principal does not only determine the level of subsidies but also the price to be paid to the agent.

An output maximising non-profit organisation therefore produces an amount of $(\alpha - \chi)/(\beta + \delta)$ units and determines the price according to the inverse demand function. When unconstrained by cost considerations, a revenue maximising organisation derives its output and the ensuing price from the condition $dR/dy=0$:

$$y^* = \alpha/2\beta$$

This is clearly smaller than α/β, but does this output level also meet the viability condition? It can easily be seen that this is the case as long as $\alpha \geq 2\beta\chi/(\beta-\delta)$. We then have a 'demand constrained' output: increasing prices causes demand to decrease in a revenue reducing way. If $\alpha < 2\beta\chi/(\beta-\delta)$ an output of $y^* = \alpha/2\beta$ would entail revenues to be lower than costs. As $dR/dy > 0$ for $y < \alpha/2\beta$, we should look for the highest possible value of y meeting the viability condition. This is clearly

$$y^* = (\alpha - \chi)/(\beta + \delta)$$

Output is 'budget constrained'.

In both cases, demand constrained output and budget constrained output, the optimal price is

$$P^* = \alpha - \beta y^*$$

Cases with price discrimination and subsidies can be analysed within a comparable approach (Niskanen 1997: 84 ff and 87 ff).

Volunteers

Some generalities

Voluntary work can be defined as 'work without monetary pay or legal obligations provided for persons outside the volunteer's own household' (Anheier 2005: 219). Mostly, but not necessarily, there is no formal contract between the volunteer and the organisation for which he performs some tasks. In some cases, volunteers, if we may call them so, are recruited through employee volunteering programmes set up in the context of Corporate Social Responsibility actions initiated by a profit organisation (Muthure *et al.* 2009). They will not be discussed here.

Data summarised by Anheier (2005: 83-85) show that in a large number of countries a significant proportion of the adult population is engaged in voluntary work, with percentages up to more than 40 per cent. Boraas (2003: 3) states that, during 2000-2001, more than 27 per cent of the US population was engaged in institutional volunteering, with a median value of 52 hours a year (*ibid*.: 7).[5]

The data presented by Anheier (2005: 83-85) also show that a large number of non-profit organisations rely to a large extent on voluntary work: on average 40 per cent of total full time equivalent (paid and unpaid) jobs in a 35 countries sample, with 75 per cent as the maximum value observed. Handy and Srinivasan (2004), for example, describe the situation in 31 Ontario hospitals (Canada), where on average 700 volunteers are active, requiring, on average again, 3.4 paid staff members to manage them, and Mook *et al.* (2007: 65)[6] even report a Canadian organisation having 121,982 volunteers, the sample median being 50 volunteers. Only about one quarter of their sampled organisations employed a volunteer manager, half of them on a full-time basis (Mook *et al.* 2007: 64).

At the board level, Smith and Shen (1996: 272) show that, in the US, almost eight times more non-profit organisations are volunteer managed, as compared to professionally managed organisations. Clearly, the latter are much larger.

Comparing the last three papers referred to leads to the insight that assuming volunteers to be a homogeneous group of people in terms of style or motives is at best a very stylised representation of reality.[7] Furthermore, as observed by Reed and Selbee (2000) and the references therein, volunteers differ significantly from non-volunteers in a number of important socio-economic and psychological aspects, as also illustrated for the latter by Frey and Götte (1999), who observe for a sample of 691 Swiss volunteers changes in the intrinsic/extrinsic motivation balance once they are rewarded financially: giving volunteers a small financial reward reduced the amount of voluntary hours performed, and that number increased again only after the payment had been increased.[8]

From a marketing point of view, it is useful to fully understand a person's decision to become a volunteer. It is almost tautological to state that a person becomes a volunteer once he perceives benefits[9] to be higher than costs. The literature reviewed by Chinman and Wandersman (1999) leads them to group volunteering benefits and costs in four categories: material benefits/costs, social benefits/costs, benefits/costs related to the organisational mission, and specific benefits/costs (Chinman and Wandersman 1999: 48 ff). As far as benefits are concerned, social and mission related benefits seem to be the most important

---

5   Institutional volunteering can defined as 'volunteering ... through organisations or groups' (Katz and Rosenberg 2005: 432), and is known to be the predominant mode of volunteering in the developed world (*ibid.*).

6   661 Canadian non-profit organisations in all kinds of industries (online survey in 2004).

7   For a review of the relevant literature, see Dolnicar and Randle (2007: 138-141), who also present an empirical motivations based segmentation of 4,267 Australian volunteers with data relating to the year 2000; see also Handy *et al.* (2000) and Hustinx (2005: 626).

8   See also Chapter 5 in the section on performance based remuneration schemes.

9   In utility terms when volunteering is considered a normal good 'consumed' by the volunteer, or in monetary terms when volunteering is seen as an investment good (Menchik and Weisbrod 1987: 161-168). We stick to the utility interpretation, all the more because we can easily interpret monetary values in a utility framework.

(*ibid.*: 55), whereas the relative importance of the cost categories seems not to be clear-cut.

In the approach of Handy *et al.* (2000: 48) perceived benefits are grouped into private benefits (B_p) and social benefits (B_s), whereas all costs (K) are assumed to be private. For somebody to become a volunteer the following condition must hold:

$$B_p + B_s > K$$

or

$$K - B_p < B_s$$

The perceived net private cost ($K - B_p$) therefore must be inferior to the social benefit as reflected by the volunteer's utility in order for a potential volunteer to become a volunteer, or superior to the social benefits in case he decides not to become a volunteer. Sundeen *et al.* (2007) concentrate on the last case, and try to determine which factors decisively affect the net private costs.[10] Three important factors emerge: time, interest, and health (Sundeen *et al.* 2007: 290), whereas other factors (child care facilities, reimbursement of expenses, the availability of better information, the existence of an employer volunteer programme, or a better skills-activity match) did not substantially increase the non-volunteers' willingness to volunteer.

Volunteering for religious organisations might imply an additional argument in the volunteer's utility function: 'afterlife utility' (Tao and Yeh 2007: 773), compounded in the overall expected utility of (religiously) volunteering, apart from its direct effect on his worldly life well-being. Controlling for devotion and a number of more traditional control variables, Tao and Yeh (2007) establish[11] a significantly positive relationship between the amount of expected rewards in the afterlife according to their religion,[12] suggesting that afterlife considerations play a role when deciding on volunteering in religious organisations.

From the organisation's point of view two issues should be raised. In the first place there is the question which tasks will be taken up by volunteers, and which by paid staff. Theoretically this is a problem of optimising the input combination, taking into consideration factors such as productivity, cost, supply, substitutes, mission, and legal obligations (Handy *et al.* 2008: 77). Handy *et al.* (2008: 87) establish[13] that on average about 13 per cent of the tasks to be performed in these organisations are open for both volunteers and paid staff, whereas about two-thirds of the tasks are only performed by paid professionals.

---

10 Sample compiled by the US Bureau of Labor Statistics in 2002, composed by 23,144 volunteers and 48,168 non-volunteers.
11 1,278 Taiwanese individuals (1999).
12 Christian religions implying a 'longer' afterlife than Buddhist religions (*ibid.*: 783).
13 428 Canadian organisations (2005) from different industries.

The second organisational issue is the fact that the presence of volunteers is not always a blessing, as it can be the source of conflicts: the volunteers might feel frustrated, constrained in their expected autonomy, or expecting some kind of eternal gratitude, whereas the employed staff sometimes consider the volunteers to be dilettantes, careless or stubborn people, or snobs.[14] To avoid such kind of conflicts, also volunteers are to be managed professionally, as in the Ontario example mentioned above. This includes investments to attract volunteers, to recruit them, and to design unequivocal expectations as to volunteers' tasks and responsibilities. The recruitment 'procedure' frequently consists of asking a person to become a volunteer, after some implicit or explicit selection procedure. Apparently, being asked to be a volunteer results in the majority of cases in a decision to become a volunteer, whereas only a minority of people not asked volunteer (71 per cent and 25 per cent respectively[15]). Even if one takes into consideration the fact that the persons asked to volunteer are not chosen at random, but might be selected because of their assumed propensity to volunteer, this effect remains, albeit to a lesser extent, the difference being 29 per cent in Yörük's sample[16] (Yörük 2008).

Voluntary board members

In Chapter 5 we have discussed the role of the board. Here we delve into the motives of potential voluntary board members for entering the board, paraphrasing a model by Handy (1995).

The potential board member is of course a utility maximiser (U_b), his utility being affected by his wealth (W) and reputation (Rep), however defined, which are substitutes: $\partial^2 U_b / \partial W \partial \text{Rep} < 0$. The standard assumption of decreasing marginal utilities also applies here: $\partial U_b / \partial W > 0$, $\partial^2 U_b / \partial W^2 < 0$, $\partial U_b / \partial \text{Rep} > 0$, and $\partial^2 U_b / \partial \text{Rep}^2 < 0$. Before joining the board the potential board member has a reputation level Rep°. If the organisation is successful after he effectively joins the board, his reputation level increases to Rep⁺, if not it decreases to Rep⁻. The probability of being successfull is s. For a given level of wealth, the corresponding utility levels are U_b^0, U_b^+, and U_b^- respectively. Therefore, the expected change in utility when joining the board is

$$sU_b^+ + (1-s)\, U_b^- - U_b^0$$

The board is only joined if this expression is positive, or

$$s > \frac{U_b^0 - U_b^-}{U_b^+ - U_b^-} = \hat{s} \tag{7.1}$$

---

14 That such perceptions are not always present is shown in the case of 270 US animal care employees, who overall had a quite positive assessment of their experiences with volunteers (Rogelberg *et al.* 2010: 434).

15 Independent Sector (US) survey during the year 2000, referred to by Sundeen *et al.* (2007: 280).

16 4,216 US adults (2001).

The more reputation the potential voluntary board member has to lose, the lower the probability he will enter the board, as this implies that the numerator of (7.1) will increase, increasing the required probability of success s. This amounts to say that asking people with higher initial reputation levels to enter a board will result in a positive answer only for high enough values of s.

What about the impact of wealth? In Appendix VII the condition for $\partial s/\partial W < 0$ is determined. If it applies this means that wealthier people will be more inclined to join the board of a non-profit organisation as a volunteer than less wealthy people, as their required level of probability of success is lower. No doubt this is also observed in the real world (Handy 1995: 300-301), though a selection mechanism might be a plausible explanation too.

The empirical literature on motives to enter a non-profit board as a volunteer is scanty and concentrates on factors other than the ones discussed in Handy's model. A review is provided by Inglis and Cleave (2006), who subsequently develop a scale to assess voluntary board member motivations. They discern[17] six dimensions for these motivations: enhancement of self-worth, individual growth, helping the community, networking, providing unique contributions to the board, and psychological self-healing (*ibid.*: 93-96).

Commitment of voluntary board members is empirically studied by Stephens *et al.* (2004)[18] connecting in a LISREL analysis affective commitment, normative commitment, and continuance commitment (commitment as a result of the comparison of perceived volunteering costs and perceived volunteering benefits; see the previous section on these) to self-reported performance.

The value of voluntary labour

It is not because voluntary labour is unpaid, that is has no value: time spent on voluntary work cannot be spent otherwise, and therefore engenders an opportunity cost. Of course, voluntary labour also results in benefits, the value of which should equal its cost in a perfectly competitive equilibrium. Because this last condition is not met in most situations where voluntary labour is observed, it is extremely difficult to estimate both its costs and benefits correctly. This results in confusion about the correct interpretation of figures made publicly available, let alone if integrated in some form of financial reporting (see also Chapter 8).

Nevertheless, valuing voluntary work is important. It has a long tradition in the context of cost-effectiveness studies, cost-utility studies, or cost-benefit studies to assess new treatments or pharmaceuticals (Drummond *et al.* 1987: Chapter 2). Therefore, it is not surprising that the most comprehensive microeconomic analysis of the valuation of voluntary work to date is made in a health economics context (Posnett and Jan 1996).

The analysis departs from a perfectly competitive equilibrium, in which the following three microeconomic principles, stemming from the optimality

---

17 220 observations of voluntary board members in a Canadian region.
18 616 board members of US Chambers of Commerce.

condition that marginal revenues need to be equal to marginal costs, hold true:

- the output price (P) equals the marginal value of output for the consumer;
- wages (w) equal the value of the marginal product of labour;
- wages also equal the marginal value of leisure time.

In a first part of the analysis voluntary labour is a substitute for paid labour, resulting in a reduction of goods or services produced (Δy), and hence a reduction in consumption, unless some compensating production is provided. The value of the production lost is $P\Delta y$, which, according to the second principle, is linked to w. If there is a compensating production, somebody has to sacrifice leisure time, the unit value of which is also w, according to the third principle. Posnett and Jan enrich their analysis by taking into consideration utility derived from labour, unemployment, taxes, and non-competitive market structures. Their conclusions remain basically unaffected (*ibid.*: 17-18).

In the second part of their analysis voluntary labour comes at the expense of leisure time, whether or not the volunteer is unemployed. Here too, utility considerations enter the analysis, though some arbitrariness cannot be avoided when trying to determine the voluntary labour's value.

In the empirical literature on voluntary labour valuation, different methods are described and applied. Foster *et al.* (2001: Chapter 4) give an overview: besides the opportunity cost approach there are the replacement cost method,[19] and the output-based method. Handy and Srinivasan (2004: 38) also describe a method based on the value the volunteers themselves attach to their voluntary work. Bowman (2009: 495-496), concentrating on the strictly economic value of volunteers to an organisation and explicitly excluding the social value, proposes the volunteers' contribution to revenues as a measure. He also discusses (*ibid.*: 494-495) the sum of recruitment, training and supervising costs, as a lower bound on the economic value. This list already shows how cost aspects and benefit aspects tend to be conflated when dealing with voluntary work, a situation which might be to a certain extent inevitable. Further, from a practical and academic point of view, it is worrying that when different methods are applied to value the same voluntary activities, widely divergent results are obtained (Foster *et al.* 2001: 110; Handy and Srinivasan 2004: 38-39).

Subsidies and gifts

Concepts

No doubt a large number of non-profit organisations only survive because they receive all sorts of gifts, in cash or in kind. Voluntary labour, discussed in the previous section, or labour donation, discussed in Chapter 5, are examples of

---

19   The cost if the voluntary work would have been performed by paid professionals, a natural
       upper bound of the volunteers' economic value (Bowman 2009: 495).

gifts in kind (Garcia and Marcuello 2002; Rose-Ackerman 1996: 702), but there are other possibilities, such as advertising campaigns produced free of charge or at a substantially reduced price by reputed marketing agencies, use of facilities without charge, or employees of profit organisations working on behalf of non-profit organisations.

Here we will confine ourselves to cash donations,[20] which can be conditional or unconditional. Three sources of donations can be distinguished: authorities at all levels, individuals, and private organisations (both profit and non-profit). Donations by authorities, which generally will be conditional, are called subsidies. Attracting subsidies can be considered as a typical marketing activity for non-profit organisations, conceptually comparable to attracting donations from individuals or organisations. As illustrated by Hager *et al.* (2002) for the US, a non-profit organisation can organise the fundraising and subsidy seeking tasks in different ways (Hager *et al.* 2002: 312-314): concentrate them with specific staff or volunteers, possibly supported by external consultants,[21] making a number of members of the organisation partly responsible for fundraising, doing nothing (as in the case of sufficient recurrent grants), outsourcing the fundraising function (in which case a transaction cost analysis would help to understand this decision), be it to a professional fundraiser (which was the case in 8 per cent of the authors' sample[22] (*ibid.*: 320)) or to a grant making charity such as United Way.

Finally, note that in a large number of countries private donations also carry a subsidy component in that they can be deducted from the donor's taxable income: part of the donation is therefore borne by the authorities, through a lessening in the amount of fiscal revenues.

Subsidies

Subsidy design when subsidiser and non-profit organisations share the same objectives

If non-profit organisations want to be eligible for subsidies, they have to conform to the conditions implied by the subsidy legislation or regulations. Sometimes these might entail some kind of moral dilemma, when the conditions are not (completely) in line with the organisation's values. Consider for example an organisation being very much in favour of labour management, confronted with a legal rule that the organisation's board must be exclusively or in majority composed by persons not employed by the organisation in order to receive subsidies. In such cases, the organisation's decision makers have to weigh principles against resources enabling them to pursue the organisation's objectives. Note that there are organisations, some of which are fairly large

---

20   Some purely financing aspects will be discussed in Chapter 9, and the role of donors as one of the organisation's principals in a principal-agent context is referred to in Chapter 5.

21   Marudas and Jacobs (2010) document a fundraising revenues enhancing impact of these, in a 2000-2001 sample of 774 US organisations (partially) outsourcing fundraising.

22   1,540 US organisations surveyed in 2001.

and well known such as Amnesty International,[23] which refuse to receive any subsidy, driven by the principle they have to maximally safeguard (the perception of) their total independence from whatever authority they might be forced by circumstances to criticize because of its human rights policy.

In theory, a subsidising authority can search for an optimal subsidy design by taking into consideration expected organisational behaviour. Duizendstraal and Nentjes (1994) provide a model in which the organisational objectives coincide with the objectives favored by the subsidising authority, but where the organisation might divert some of the resources to undesirable destinations ('slack'), such as too high wages, perks, or activities not contributing to reach organisational goals (Duizendstraal and Nentjes 1994: 298). There are no agency problems between the organisation's board and its management.

Define y_d as the amount of desirable output, and y_s as the amount of slack. Organisational utility is U, concave in y_d and y_s. The organisation's problem then is

$$\max_{y_d, y_s} U(y_d, y_s)$$

Costs are separable in both outputs, convex in y_d and proportional to y_s, the proportionality factor being c_s:

$$C = C_d(y_d) + C_s(y_s)$$

with $\partial C_d/\partial y_d > 0$, $\partial^2 C_d/\partial y_d^2 \geq 0$, $\partial C_s/\partial y_s > 0$, and $\partial^2 C_s/\partial y_s^2 = 0$.

Note that it is assumed that that there is no fixed cost in producing slack. It is also assumed that only C is observable, and not its components.

Only desired output generates revenues $R = P(y_d)y_d$, and the organisation is modelled to break even after taking into consideration subsidies S:

$$S + R = C$$

Subsidies can take different forms, four of which are analysed by Duizendstraal and Nentjes (1994):
- a lump sum subsidy ($S = S_{ls}$);
- a subsidy based on the value of inputs ($S = sC$);
- a subsidy based on the amount of the desired output ($S = gy_d$);
- a subsidy based on the revenues generated by the desired output ($S = tR$).

It goes without saying that the parameters s, g and t are (strictly) positive. Setting s>1 would be illogical, as it makes it impossible for the break even condition to hold. In cases where $(C_d(y_d) - R) > R$, t should be greater than 1,

---

23   In some countries, such as Flanders (Belgium), they accept subsidies, though not directly from national governments (www.aivl.be; consulted in January 2011).

otherwise it would be impossible for the organisation to break even. This case is not unrealistic, as numerous organisations provide their goods or services at very low, or even nominal, prices. Note that when goods or services are delivered free of charge, a revenue based subsidy is not an option.

As is shown in Appendix VIII, each subsidy regime implies a relationship between the desired output and slack $y_d(y_s)$, reducing the organisational maximisation problem to

$$\max_{y_d} U(y_d, y_s(y_d))$$

The first-order condition for a maximum is

$$dU/dy_d = \partial U/\partial y_d + \partial U/\partial y_s \, dy_s/dy_d = 0$$

from which the traditional condition

$$dy_s/dy_d = - (\partial U/\partial y_d)/(\partial U/\partial y_s)$$

In Appendix VIII (parts 1-4) the optimality conditions along the four 'pseudo-transformation' curves $y_s(y_d)$ (one for each subsidy regime) are derived (accents representing (partial) derivatives with respect to quantity):
- under a lump sum subsidy: $dy_s/dy_d = (R' - C_d')/c_s$
- under an input value based subsidy: $dy_s/dy_d = (R' - (1\text{-}s) \, C_d')/(1\text{-}s)c_s$
- under an output quantity based subsidy: $dy_s/dy_d = (R' - C_d' + g)/c_s$
- under a revenue based subsidy: $dy_s/dy_d = (R'(1\text{+}t) - C_d')/c_s$

The subsidising authority should take this behaviour into consideration when designing subsidy schemes. Its objective might be efficiency (maximising y_d/y_s) or just maximising y_d. The exact forms of the demand function and the cost functions will determine which subsidy type is optimal, as a closer look at the different shapes of $y_s(y_d)$ and the ensuing optimality conditions shows that none of the four subsidy regimes studied dominates all the others.

Subsidy design when subsidiser and non-profit organisations do not share the same objectives

Whereas the previous section deals with a situation in which both the subsidising authority and the non-profit organisation agree upon the desired output, but in which the organisation has some preference for the production of slack, there are also cases where there is no complete agreement upon the desired output. Designing subsidy schemes therefore implies taking into consideration their incentive effects, a problem central in principal-agent theories. Here, the principal is the subsidising authority, and the organisation is the agent. Though the mathematical aspects of these theories are interesting in their own right, it is also useful to have an incentive based typology of subsidy schemes in mind when theorising about them. Due to the long-standing budgetary problems related to the provision of health care, such a typology has been developed in the literature of health care financing systems. It is easily generalised to all subsidised sectors, as will become clear in the following paragraphs (based on Jegers *et al.* (2002)).

The first of the two important dimensions of an incentive based typology of subsidy systems is the distinction between fixed systems and variable systems, the difference being that fixed systems are independent of activity levels, whereas variable systems are not. Financing systems which are fixed at the organisational level clearly provide incentives to reduce marginal costs, since marginal revenues are zero. This can be done in different ways, e.g. by reducing output levels and/or quality levels, as long as regulatory benchmarks are not breached. Financing systems fixed at the macro level are called *closed-end* systems (the others being *open-end* systems). They consist of a budgetary cap at the industry level, making budgeting easy for the authorities, but life difficult for the subsidised organisations, as, from their point of view, they will experience uncertainty as to the revenues they are entitled to as long as the allocation of the macro budget has not been decided upon. In systems variable at the organisational level, funding depends on the amount of output produced by the organisation. Incentives depend on the balance between marginal revenues and marginal costs, with generous per unit subsidies generating (too) high activity levels. Mostly these systems will be open-end systems, but if they are of the closed-end type, and therefore fixed at the macro level, it is not only the own organisational activity level that will determine the subsidies the organisation will receive, but also the levels generated by the other subsidised organisations. In such a situation, systematically increasing production levels does not guarantee an increase in revenues. This will only be the case if an organisation's activity level grows faster that the other providers' aggregate output level.

The second dimension of subsidy schemes is the distinction between *retrospective* funding systems and *prospective* systems. In a retrospective system the organisation's costs are subsidised (fully or partially) taking into consideration actual expenses, and is therefore an *ex-post* system. This is clearly not an effective mechanism to contain costs. In prospective systems subsidies per unit of activity are determined *ex-ante*. In that sense a fixed budget at the organisational level can be called a prospective payment system in which the unit is the organisation itself. Prospective systems encourage efficiency, as financial profits stemming from the difference between the subsidy per unit of subsidy and the cost per unit of subsidy remain within the organisation, enabling it to expand activities, increase quality of provision, or serve clients in great financial need. On the other hand, skimming might be a risk, organisations only accepting clients of which they know the cost they generate will be relatively low, necessitating some kind of quality and accessibility control.

In practice, most subsidy systems are not pure in the sense that they can be unequivocally described by determining whether they are fixed or variable, and whether they are prospective or retrospective, considering the appropriate unit of payment. Therefore, they are labelled *hybrid* systems, with interacting, and sometimes counteracting, incentive mechanisms. Different modes of hybridisation within one industry can be distinguished:[24] different subsidisers apply different systems, different systems apply to different categories of providers, different systems apply for different categories of costs or investments, and finally subsidisers mix themselves features of the different generic systems into their subsidy schemes.

Donations by individuals: the optimal level of fundraising

Without any doubt, effective fundraising starts with a thorough knowledge of the relevant characteristics of potential donors, appropriately segmenting the 'donor market' in order to increase the efficiency of the organisation's fundraising efforts, and correctly differentiating policies between donor recruitment campaigns and donor development activities (Sargeant 2005: 214-234). A number of descriptive papers on donation behaviour are available, mostly pertaining to the US: Hewitt and Brown (2000: 168-170) provide a review of this literature up to 1996, while other examples of papers worth mentioning are by Apinunmahakul *et al.* (2009; with Canadian data), Brooks (2005), Havens *et al.* (2006), James and Sharpe (2007), Okten and Weisbrod (2000), Tinkelman (2004), the multidisciplinary review by Sargeant and Woodliffe (2008), and Sargeant *et al.* (2006) who specifically deal with legacy pledgers. An overview of econometric problems in such studies is provided by Bakija and Heim (2008: 1-2): the difficulty of separately identifying price (of donation; see below) and income effects, the confounding of transitory and permanent changes in price and income, the difficulty to control for all relevant unobservables, and the assumption of parameter homogeneity across individuals. Donations to religious organisations are studied by Tao and Yeh (2007). In their Taiwanese sample described earlier in the section on volunteering they also observe a significantly positive link between the amount of donations and the amount of expected rewards in the afterlife according to the donor's religion[25] (Tao and Yeh 2007: 782). It is also noted that, in their sample, religious volunteering and religious donations seem to be substitutes for one another (*ibid.*: 783).

Besides the personal characteristics of the potential donors, competition on the donor market also has a bearing on the eventual amount of donations an organisation will raise (Bilodeau, Slivinski 1997).

From an economic point of view, the standard assumption with respect to donors is that they are 'impurely altruistic', in the sense that they value, in utility terms, three items: their own wealth, the realisation of the cause

---

24 Jegers *et al.* (2002: 269-271) present examples of each in a health care context.
25 Christian religions implying a 'longer' afterlife than Buddhist religions, folk religions promising no afterlife at all.

for which they donate, and the act of giving itself (the 'warm glow' effect) (Andreoni 1990: 465).

An often proposed criterion to compare the ultimate use made of one unit of currency by an organisation receiving donations is the 'price' of donations: the outlay of the donor net of personal tax advantages $(F(1-t)^{26})$, divided by the programme costs, which are assumed to be spent on activities promoting the objectives of the organisation $(C - A - f$; with C for total costs, A for administrative costs exclusive of fundraising costs, and f for fundraising costs; the tax rate is assumed to be given[27]):

$$\frac{F(1-t)}{C-A-f}$$

The literature reviews by Parsons (2003: 115) and Jacobs and Marudas (2009: 34-40) show that donations, admittedly from all kinds of sources, in general are negatively correlated with this price variable.[28] The results obtained by Brooks (2007),[29] focusing on the specific impact of tax rates, point in the same direction, adding the insight that price elasticities significantly differ between the kinds of activities the receiving organisations are engaged in (Brooks 2007: 609). Tinkelman (1998)[30] shows that larger donors are more sensitive to donation price indicators than smaller donors. A comparable result is found by Tinkelman and Mankaney (2007),[31] who conclude that the efficiency sensitivity of donations (efficiency proxied here by $A/(C-f)$) is only an issue when efficiency data are both reliable and relevant (Tinkelman and Mankaney 2007: 54). More detailed results are described by Bakija and Heim (2008: 41).[32] They show permanent income elasticities to be more prominent than transitory income elasticities, and persistent price elasticities to be larger for high-income earners.

Despite the observed relationship between donations and donation prices, which might partly be induced by the availability and frequent use of watchdog standards which include price in one way or another (Bhattacharya and Tinkelman 2009),[33] there are a number of conceptual problems with the donation

---

26   It might include the avoided capital gain taxes on gifts of appreciated assets, as in Bakija and Heim (2008: 10).

27   See Kaplow (1995) for a theoretical analysis of the socially optimal tax-exemption rate for gifts.

28   See also Gordon and Khumawala (1999: 47) for a limited literature review, and Marudas and Jacobs (2004) for an econometrically subtle empirical study on 1,014 US non-profit organisations for 1985–1994.

29   4,406 US families for the year 2000.

30   The 1991 and 1992 donations for 191 large New York non-profit organisations with education programmes.

31   Essentially on a 2000-2001 sample of 469,525 US non-profit organisations, the results of which are compared with a restricted sample of 27,602 of these organisations.

32   294,513 US observations for 1979-2005.

33   Silvergleid (2003: 11-16) provides an overview of US watchdog agencies, and finds mixed results as to their impact on donations, contrary to Gordon *et al.* (2009) who report a positive correlation between rate changes and both donation levels and changes on a sample of 405

price variable, apart from the accounting manipulation possibilities which are discussed in the next chapter, and the debatable underlying assumption that potential donors correctly assess the variables involved. Bennett and Savani (2003), for instance, document that a sample of 286 potential donors estimate 46 per cent of the costs of four well-known UK non-profit organisations to reach beneficiaries, whereas the actual amount is 82 per cent (Bennett and Savani 2003: 337).

A first conceptual problem is the observation that only programme expenses are taken into consideration, but not output itself, ignoring possible efficiency differences between organisations (Parsons 2003: 114). The second is that, from a theoretical point of view, average values are bad guides when it comes to identify the organisation to which an additional donation would result in a maximal increase of output, even though in practice marginal activities are difficult, if not impossible, to determine. The last point is that fully subtracting administrative costs and fundraising costs is not really appropriate, as a certain amount of administration is necessary to make programme activities possible, as are fundraising efforts to raise funds. The mere presence of these costs is not an indication of inefficiency. Of course, there can be too much (but also too little) fundraising costs or administrative costs, in that they have a negative impact on the total amount of activities the organisation can fund. The paper by Kähler and Sargeant (2002) is an example of a benchmarking exercise for the A/C ratio (administration costs to total expenditures),[34] taking into consideration a size effect, which is natural to expect as (a large) part of the administration costs are fixed. For anecdotic reference, the highest value of A/C observed in their sample was an astonishingly high 0.43 (Kähler and Sargeant 2002: 221). Castaneda *et al.* (2008: 238-243) shed additional light on this efficiency issue by establishing[35] a negative relationship between administrative expenses and the level of competition on the market. Finally, Jacobs and Marudas (2009) argue[36] that the efficiency variable A/C and the price variable C/(C–A–f) should be considered simultaneously when modelling donation levels, taking into consideration industry effects (Jacobs and Marudas 2009: 48).

Combining personal characteristics of the potential donors, competition on the donor market, possibly intensified by the availability of accountability ratings (Chen 2009, Sloan 2009), together with other potential factors such as the design of the fundraising campaign (Karlan and List 2007, Landry *et al.* 2006, Lange and Stocking 2009, Van Diepen *et al.* 2009), makes it theoretically possible to derive a fundraising function F(f) at the organisational level, describing the relationship between fundraising expenses (f) and the funds collected. Two opposing effects are at work here. There is a positive one due to

---

organisations receiving at least yearly 500,000 USD public support followed by the US based Charity Navigator (website data retrieved in 2007).

34   410 British and Welsh charities out of the top 500 fundraising charities (aggregated data for 1992-1996).

35   24,047 local US non-profit organisations in 2,252 markets in 16 industries (cross-sectional data for 2000).

36   US sample of 5,493 organisations (2000-2001) in five industries.

the reduction of the information cost for potential donors, and a negative one (at least in a static sense) as each unit of currency used for fundraising cannot be used for output production (making the price of a donation higher) (Okten and Weisbrod 2000: 257).

The question now is to determine the optimal level of fundraising. In Chapter 5, Steinberg's (1986b) model was presented as a method to gauge the distance, in terms of objectives, between the organisational board and its manager. Here we will use the same kind of model, but from a slightly different perspective, to determine the optimal level of fundraising. The balance between principals and agent is assumed to be fixed, leading to an organisational utility function that is a weighted average of service maximisation (preferred by the principals), and budget maximisation (preferred by the agent), the weighting factor being k $(0 \leq k \leq 1)$, where k=0 describes a situation of pure budget maximisation, and k=1 represents a situation of pure service maximisation (S is the level of subsidies, not affected by the amount of funds raised, and R stands for the other revenues):

$$U_{npo} = k(R+S+F(f)-f-A) + (1-k)(R+S+F(f)) = R+S+F(f) - k(A+f)$$

Taking the first derivative with respect to f leads to the (first-order) optimality condition

$$dF/df = k \qquad (7.2)$$

or, expressed as an elasticity,

$$\frac{dF/F}{df/f} = kf/F$$

The Brooks-Ondrich (2007) formulation of the organisational utility function, discussed in Chapter 5, leads to a slightly more complex first order condition for $\partial F/\partial f$ than (7.2) (to be derived from (II.1) in Appendix II).

Tinkelman (2006), acknowledging the fact that in practice determining marginal values such as dF/df is difficult, if not impossible, evaluates whether average historical values (of the type F/f) are good proxies. His conclusion[37] is that 'average historic ratios are not an appropriate proxy for marginal fundraising rations' (*ibid.*: 461).

Assuming F(f) to be concave, Thornton (2006) infers that entry on the donor market would reduce the marginal effect of the fundraising efforts, resulting in lower optimal fundraising efforts at the organisational level, as the parameter k in (7.2) is unaffected.[38] But as the number of organisations increases, one can wonder how the aggregate fundraising costs would change. If there would be an increase, as is the case in his sample of about 30,000 local US non-profit

---

37 1982-1994 panel of 2,430 US organisations providing higher education.
38 The same conclusion can be reached when assuming a Brooks-Ondrich (2007) organisational utility function.

organisations for the period 1990-2000, there might be a social cost that could be avoided if an entry preventing or reducing regulation were in place.

Donations by firms

The question why firms, and not their owners, donate to non-profit organisations,[39] is still an unresolved matter, both in normative writings and in descriptive studies: '[r]esearchers cannot agree on the motives, and commentators cannot agree on what ought to motivate philanthropic collaborations. To complicate matters one often finds different motives in the same firm, and sometimes in the same executives.' (Galaskiewicz and Sinclair Colman 2006: 185). Probably, a universally valid motive just does not exist, as motives will depend on factors such as circumstances, psychological diversity of the actors involved, and/or opportunities. A good illustration of this, though there might be some problems of socially desirably answering, is the work by Meijer *et al.* (2006). A large majority of their respondents[40] indicated to have only one motive for sponsoring or giving. Strangely enough, even for sponsoring the most frequently mentioned most important motive was social involvement (38 per cent of respondents in the last year surveyed), followed by commercial motives (29 per cent). These percentages change to 56 per cent and 7 per cent respectively for charitable giving (Meijer *et al.* 2006: 20-21).

Though Galaskiewicz and Sinclair Colman (2006: 185-195) discern six categories of motives for corporate philanthropy (which is broader a concept than mere donations) in their extensive review of the empirical literature, these categories can be aggregated in two non mutually exclusive groups as far as donation motives are concerned (Aralumpalam and Stoneman 1995: 938): shareholders' wealth maximisation,[41] and managerial utility maximisation.[42] Maximising shareholders' wealth can be achieved by positively affecting the firm's profit, for example through the creation of public goodwill with respect to the firm,[43] but also by donating to causes to which the shareholders themselves would donate, taking advantage of differences in tax deductibility between corporate donations and private donations. In these cases, managers are perfect agents. Agency conflicts arise when managers donate to beneficiaries they personally like, ignoring their shareholders' preferences (Navarro 1988: 70-76). A very special case of managerial utility increasing donations is the use of corporate foundations, which possibly serve causes supported by the firm's owners, but to which discretionary payments are made as part of an earnings management policy, without necessarily jeopardising the stability of the foundation's disbursements.

---

39 We do not consider sponsorship, as it implies some reciprocity between the sponsoring firm and the organisation sponsored (Sargeant 2005: 235).
40 Between 998 and 1,122 Dutch firms (1995-2003) on their giving behaviour.
41 Special cases of which are the following groups of Galaskiewicz and Sinclair Colman (2006: 188-195): strategic collaboration, commercial collaboration, and political collaboration.
42 Including the pursuit of social welfare (Galaskiewicz and Sinclair Colman 2006: 188).
43 For an early model, see Navarro (1988: 67-70).

Data presented by Petrovits (2006)[44] are consistent with the existence of this kind of behaviour, which can be labelled as 'real' earning manipulations, as opposed to 'accounting' manipulations (see Chapter 8).

An empirical strategy to discriminate between a perfect agent situation and an imperfect agent situation is to look at changes in corporate donations when corporate tax rates change. The idea is that under the hypothesis of the firm acting in the interest of its owners, increasing corporate tax rates would decrease the relative price of corporate donations as compared to private donations by the owners. Increasing corporate donations should then be expected, whereas utility maximising managers would decrease the amount of corporate donations, as long as the marginal managerial utility with respect to (net) donations is smaller in absolute value than the marginal managerial utility with respect to (net) profits. The results of Aralumpalam and Stoneman (1995)[45] indeed show rising donations when corporate taxes increase, which is in line with the perfect agent point of view. A comparable conclusion is reached by Carroll and Joulfaian (2005). Their analysis is cross-sectional.[46]

Brown *et al.* (2006) follow another empirical strategy to distinguish between the two groups of motives. They build on the idea that if weaker governance structures are in place, imperfect agents will feel free to pursue private utility maximisation. Therefore, establishing a link between looser governance mechanisms and corporate giving points at the presence of imperfect agents as far as donating is concerned. Their (cross-sectional) results[47] are compatible with this. Larger firms with larger boards and lower levels of debt are more inclined to donate. Note that this conclusion is opposite to the one of the tax effect studies discussed in the previous paragraph, confirming the opening citation of this section.

Notwithstanding the motives leading to corporate charity, there is empirical support to state that it brings corporate benefits with it.[48] Furthermore, Lichtenstein *et al.* (2004) observe an increase in private donations by the customers of 'socially responsible' firms to the non-profit organisations these firms are visibly linked with.

Marx (1999) addresses the position of corporate philanthropy in the corporate strategic planning process. His data[49] allow him to conclude that 'companies are increasingly integrating philanthropic management into the formal strategic planning of the firm' (Marx 1999: 185), rather pointing at a profit maximising role of corporate philanthropy, though 'strategic philanthropy

---

44   323 of the larger US corporate foundations (1989-2000).
45   53 UK firms for the period 1979-1986.
46   More than 26,000 US firms for 1991.
47   701 firm-years based on data of 207 Fortune 500 (US) firms for a time frame ending in 1999.
48   Lichtenstein *et al.* (2004), based on a field survey of 1,000 (US) customers and three follow-up laboratory experiments; Lev *et al.* (2010) who find, controlling for all possible confounding factors, corporate donations causing revenue growth in subsequent years, on 1,618 (US) firm-year observations between 1989 and 2000).
49   226 large US companies (1993).

programmes do not frequently measure the direct impact of contributions to business goals' (*ibid.*: 191). Furthermore, the majority of firms did not seem to bother to assess the final destination of their donations.

Interactions between gifts and subsidies

When developing strategies in order to maximise gifts and subsidies, one should not ignore the possibility that both are connected in one way or another. There are at least four mechanisms through which this can happen.

The first one is an internal one, described by Andreoni and Payne (2003) and Brooks (2005: 553): obtaining subsidies could result in less managerial efforts to raise other kinds of funds, either spontaneously or forced by the subsidy rules. Andreoni and Payne (2003: 793-797) present a theoretical model to understand this effect. It is based on the idea that fundraising generates organisational disutility, reducing the optimal level of fundraising when subsidies increase. This effect is also observed in their sample[50] (Andreoni and Payne 2003: 797-799, 807). Song and Yi (2011) find in a stochastic frontier model applied to art organisations[51] that receiving more subsidies goes together with a reduction of fundraising efficiency,[52] which on its turn leads to less gifts received. This result is compatible with the efforts mechanism described above.

The next two mechanisms are external: higher subsidies can make donors less inclined to continue to donate, as they perceive their gifts to be less necessary (*crowding out*), but can as well attract new donations, if obtaining subsidies is considered to be a signal of the organisation's reliability and trustworthiness (*crowding in*). The two effects are not mutually exclusive, and their combined effect (together with the possible effect of the internal mechanism) is not *a priori* constant across industries (Smith 2007: 139) or across different subsidy levels. This last point is illustrated by Borgonovi (2006):[53] at low subsidy levels she observes crowding in, whereas at higher levels, crowding out occurs (Borgonovi 2006: 443-444).

Andreoni and Payne (2011) try to assess the relative importance of crowding in/out and the decreasing fundraising effort on donations[54] and conclude that 'the bulk of [the decrease in donations] is attributable to a decline in fundraising' (Andreoni and Payne 2011: 339), sometimes even reaching levels above 100 per cent,[55] depending on the estimation strategy (*ibid.*: 340).

---

50 233 art organisations and 534 social services organisations (US) receiving grants and showing fundraising activities (1992-1983 and 1985-1998, 2,417 and 4,954 observations respectively).
51 789 US art organisations (2004).
52 Except for museums and performing arts organisations.
53 404 pooled observations on 82 US non-profit theatres (1997-2001).
54 8,062 US organisations and 39,769 unbalanced panel observations (1985-2002).
55 Implying crowding in, labeled 'direct crowding in' by Andreoni and Payne (2011). They call the first mechanism 'indirect crowding out' and the second one 'direct crowding out'.

The fourth mechanism consists of private donations crowding out subsidies, as suggested on theoretical grounds by Heutel (2009), though he did not find an empirical confirmation.[56]

Tinkelman (2010) provides a thorough review of the available empirical literature with US data on crowding out and crowding in between gifts and subsidies. He concludes that there is 'no one neat, easy conclusion'(Tinkelman 2010: 37), especially not at the industry and organisational levels.

It goes without saying that crowding in and crowding out by subsidies are realistic descriptions only if donors have some background knowledge about the subsidies granted to the organisation they intend to donate to. Institutional donors can be expected to posses such knowledge, but this is not necessarily the case for individual donors: Horne *et al.* (2005) establish that in their sample[57] 45 per cent did not have any idea about the subsidies received by the organisations they donated to (and therefore had no perception, right or wrong), whereas only 28 per cent of the sample managed to make a correct estimation within 10 percent error limits.

Profit activities by non-profit organisations

Selling goods or services produced by non-profit organisations at a non-zero price is clearly more 'commercial' than delivering them free of charge, especially when the payment is to be made by the client himself, and not through some collective insurance system. Guo (2006: 125) argues that US organisations have been forced to increasingly adapt this kind of commercialisation due to the apparent decrease of the levels of donations and, more importantly, of subsidies. Pricing as such is discussed earlier in this chapter.

The commercial activities we want to discuss in this section are of a different order, as they pertain to activities not related to the organisation's mission or objectives and possibly performed through a separate profit subsidiary of the non-profit organisation,[58] with the sole aim to generate funds to finance the organisation's core activities. This implies that developing unprofitable unrelated activities negatively affects the organisation's possibilities as to these core activities (Weisbrod 1998: 16). Besides the requirement that the profit activity should generate profits, initiating such activities seems rational only if the following conditions are met (Cordes and Weisbrod 1998: 201; Tuckman 1998b: 36):

- there must be a need for additional funds;
- there is no better way than the profit activity under consideration to generate these funds;
- the activity cannot be incompatible with the organisation's values and objectives;

---

56 174,828 observations on 29,138 US organisations for 1998-2003.
57 675 donating inhabitants of the state of Georgia (US).
58 E.g. for tax related reasons (Tuckman 2009: 131).

- the organisation must be able to deliver the 'profit' output and to develop an adequate marketing plan for it;
- there must be a market for this output.

Additionally, possible crowding out effects must be taken into consideration, both of voluntary labour (Enjolras 2002) and of donors. Donors might think their donations are less necessary, or just may dislike the commercial aura within commercial activities (Young and Steinberg 1995: 161). Their attitude towards the organisation's commercialisation can be influenced by a number of elements (*ibid.*): are buyers and donors different groups, is the product sold unique, are organisations competing on the donor market also engaging in commercial activities, and the price and quality of the 'profit' good or service. An experiment by Desmet (1998) within a large French charity shows that commercial activities had a negative effect on the level of donations in the long term. Yetman and Yetman (2003) observe a partial crowding out effect in three out of the four broad non-profit industries they study.[59] A remarkable finding in their study is the fact that, in all industries, 'related' business income negatively affects private donations.

A basic economic model of a non-profit organisation engaged in profit activities is provided by Schiff and Weisbrod (1991: 621-625). In their model, there is no agency conflict between board and management, and the organisation is constrained to break even. The organisation produces a desired output y_d and a commercial output y_c. Organisational utility is $U_{np}(y_d,y_c)$, the desired output being liked, but the commercial output not being liked: $\partial U_{np}/\partial y_d > 0$, $\partial U_{np}/\partial y_c \leq 0$. The level of donations F is positively affected by the amount of desired output, and negatively by the amount of commercial output: $\partial F/\partial y_d \geq 0$, $\partial F/\partial y_c \leq 0$. The commercial output y_c is sold on a competitive market at a price P_c, whereas y_d is sold at an exogenous price P_d, which is possibly zero. Joint costs are $C(y_d,y_c)$. The maximisation problem therefore is

$$\text{Max } U_{np}(y_d,y_c)$$
$$y_d,y_c$$

$$\text{subject to: } F(y_d,y_c) + P_d y_d + P_c y_c - C(y_d,y_c) = 0$$

From Appendix IX we learn that the organisation will provide the desired output beyond the profit maximising level, whereas it will not fully take advantage of the profit generating potential of the commercial output (except if neither the donations nor the organisation's utility are affected by it: $\partial F/\partial y_c = \partial U_{np}/\partial y_c = 0$). Given the initial assumptions made as to the utility function, these conclusions are not surprising.

Bises (2000) introduces agency problems in a comparable context, though his eventual objective is to assess the appropriateness of tax exemptions on commercial profits, as opposed to subsidising y_d. Managers derive utility from

---

59   1,061 observations for 1995, US data.

making y_d available and from discretionary expenses. The commercial output y_c has neither bearing on their utilities nor on the level of donations (Bises 2000: 24, 25), assumptions automatically leading to a profit maximising production level of the commercial output, the profits being split between discretionary expenses and additional production of the desired output.

Finally, the empirical paper by Du Bois *et al.* (2004b)[60] departs from the assumption that $\partial U_m/\partial y_c > 0$. These authors expect that the more important agents are in a non-profit organisation, the more their objectives will be pursued, including more commercial activities. Potential agency conflicts are measured as the ratio between the level of directors' compensation and net assets, whereas the pursuit of managerial objectives is reflected by the level of Unrelated Business Income. After taking stock of the required control variables such as size, their conclusion does not contradict their expectations.

---

60   2,103 US non-profit organisations for the fiscal year 2000.

8 Accounting in
non-profit organisations

Introduction

Though there are no accounting concepts exclusively applicable to non-profit organisations, a specific economic theory of the presence and form of accounting in non-profit organisations has its place. Such a theory is presented in this chapter, looking at financial accounting, auditing, financial statements and their disclosure, and cost accounting. As is the case for the accounting theory developed for profit organisations, this approach is embedded in a principal-agent framework.

Principles of accounting and control

Accounting

Defining accounting as registering transactions having an impact on the organisation's wealth and periodically reporting this wealth and how it changed implies that there is no reason for the concepts and techniques of accounting to be different for non-profit organisations compared with other organisations (Anthony 1980: 84). Therefore, textbooks on accounting for non-profit organisations are perfectly comparable with accounting textbooks dealing with profit organisations, except perhaps for the examples included and elaborations on specific regulations.

Nevertheless, trying to understand why and how accounting and accounting regulations emerge in a non-profit context is a distinct economic problem, that can be dealt with within the confines of the well-established field of 'accounting and economics', which up to now has focused on these questions almost exclusively with respect to profit organisations.[1] A limited number of papers characterised by a more economic approach to accounting of non-profit

---

1   The work by Watts and Zimmerman (1986, 1990) is seminal in this domain.

organisations are available for the health care sector,[2] though the health care institution point of view mostly dominates institutional choice aspects. Most of the samples involved contain a mix of profit hospitals, public hospitals, and non-profit hospitals. A first attempt to develop a specific non-profit accounting economic theory is Jegers (2002), on which later sections of this chapter are based.

Auditing

Once again there is no reason to presume that auditors should apply specific standards and methods when auditing non-profit organisations. Clearly, the way external control is implemented might be idiosyncratic, taking into consideration industry specificities and possible (non-accounting) regulatory obligations.

The same reasoning applies when it comes to audit fees (Beattie *et al.* 2001: 249). In general, non-profit organisations are characterised by a lower litigation risk, more complex financing regulations, the presence of gifts and donations which impact on control procedures, uncertainties with respect to future income and their implications for the going concern assessment, and possibly the position of volunteers in the organisation's financial management. Frequently, the absence of performing internal control procedures complements this list as it affects the auditor's procedures and activities, and hence the auditing cost. Finally, also auditors can show some proclivity towards altruism (*ibid.*: 272), making (part of) their audit a donation in kind, in which case it is hoped that they apply the same professional standards as in fully billed audits.

Beattie *et al.* (2001) find audit fees charged to non-profit organisations[3] to be lower than for audits as comparable as possible in the profit sector. The three possible reasons for this (lower audit risk, auditor altruism, lower audit quality) cannot be disentangled. A traditional audit pricing model is also developed and tested. Two auditee characteristics positively influence audit prices (and thus monitoring costs): size, and the share of year-end stock in total assets (as an indicator of asset composition). On top of that, Big Six fees are considerably higher (18.5 per cent) than fees for other audit firms, and there is also an (albeit small on average) premium for non-Big Six audit firms with charity experience. A related study[4] is performed by Vermeer *et al.* (2009). They find a significantly positive impact on audit fees of size, (inventories + receivables)/total assets, the auditor being a Big Four firm, and financial health, and a negative impact of the share of non-audit fees in total fees. An

---

2 Early examples are Burik and Duvall 1985, Carey 1994, Eldenburg and Kallapur 1997, Eldenburg and Soderstrom 1996, Jegers and Houtman 1993, and Noreen and Soderstrom 1994.

3 More than 200 UK charities (1995 and 1997) which have to disclose audit fees and fees for non-audit services. The original sample contained more than 300 organisations, but a large number of them did not provide their financial statements, contrary to the legal obligation to do so.

4 125 out of the 1,000 largest US non-profit organisations (data on 2004).

interesting extension of the Beattie *et al.* study (2001) consists of assessing the impact of internal control quality, which is found to be positive, implying that in their sample internal control and external control are complements rather than substitutes (Vermeer *et al.* 2009: 297-298).

How are accounting and control perceived?

As has been the case for marketing (see Chapter 7), accounting and financial control have been viewed for decades as (un)necessary evils in the non-profit sector, frequently because of 'the ideological rejection of commercial values and practices' (Panozzo and Zan 1995: 8) within the organisations involved. Increasing regulatory pressures seem to have curbed this attitude, especially in larger organisations, though there still seems to be a long way to go before accounting information will be used in a non-profit setting in the same unprejudiced way as in a profit setting, accepting the fact that assessing organisational wealth does not imply maximising organisational wealth.

A consequence of the limited role attached to accounting procedures has been the absence of fully developed and effective internal control procedures in the majority of non-profit organisations: there is 'an accumulation of evidence which points to systemic and widespread failure of internal control' (Ortmann and Schlesinger 1997: 103). Currently, at least in the US, internal control systems are frequently present, as observed in the sample of Iyer and Watkins (2008) referred to in Chapter 5, where 78 per cent of the respondents claim to have formal internal control mechanisms in place (Iyer and Watkins 2008: 271).

Empirical research on internal control in non-profit organisations is scant, except for the papers by Iyer and Watkins (2008) (mentioned above) and Petrovits *et al.* (2011), and the early paper by Rayburn and Rayburn (1991), who analyse internal control reactions of 307 US hospitals to the introduction of prospective payment systems for hospital financing (see Chapter 7). The non-profit hospitals appeared to increase the tightness and centralisation of financial controls, and the use of administrative committees and ad hoc coordination groups more intensively than proprietary hospitals. Whether the explanation for this was catching up or taking the lead could not be assessed. The more recent data presented by Petrovits *et al.* (2011) reveal that only about 15 per cent of their observations[5] showed 'reportable conditions in internal controls over financial reporting' (Petrovits *et al.* 2011: 342), with less financially healthy and growing organisations showing more internal control deficiencies (*ibid*.: 345). Further, they establish 'that weak internal controls over financial reporting are negatively associated with subsequent public support and government contributions after controlling for the currrent level of support and other factors' (*ibid*.: 354).

---

5   127,988 observations on 27,495 US public charities (1999-2007) receiving federal funding of at least USD 500,000 (USD 300,000 before 2004).

Accounting theory for non-profit organisations

The framework

Assuming managerial utility in non-profit organisations is affected by both the achievement of organisational objectives (labelled 'oo' in what follows) and discretionary managerial expenses ('d') (see Chapter 5), and the non-profit board members' utilities only by the achievement of organisational objectives, information asymmetries between board and management can induce managerial behaviour that is not compatible with board utility maximisation, entailing welfare losses for the board (which is the principal). Part of the information asymmetry pertains to the financial condition of the organisation, which is (partially) affected by discretionary managerial behaviour. Even in a world without accounting regulations, an assumption that will be relaxed later on, imposing the production and audit of financial statements will mitigate this asymmetry and the ensuing residual loss at a cost, which is a monitoring cost. As long as the latter is lower than the reduction of the former, the introduction of an accounting system will improve the eventual welfare position of the board, even if, realistically, a first best situation will never obtain.

Though the same line of reasoning can be applied to deal with other principal-agent relationships, such as the relationships with donors and the organisation (Krishnan *et al.* 2006: 402), we will confine ourselves to the interplay between managers and board members. Generalising the theory presented here to other principal-agent configurations is straightforward.

In this context, religious organisations considering some deity, which, by definition, is omniscient, as the ultimate principal occupy a special position. Information asymmetry between this principal and the worldly agents cannot exist, hence accounting is useless as an information asymmetry reducing tool. In the words of Abdul-Rahman and Goddard (1998: 196): '[a]ccountability in such a world is to God and accounting can contribute little in this relationship'. If one accepts this position, religious non-profits are to be excluded from the present analysis. If not, they can be treated like any other non-profit organisation, as exemplified by Duncan *et al.* (1999) or Laughlin (1990). The latter is a so-called principal–agent analysis of the Church of England, albeit with definitions (Laughlin, 1990: 95) deviating from the Jensen–Meckling standard definitions of principals and agents (see Chapter 5).

No board: the founder is the manager

In organisations in which the founder and the manager are the same person (called in Chapter 4 the entrepreneur-manager), there is no agency problem to be solved. Defining oo_{max} to be the highest level of organisational objectives that can be attained, Figure 8.1 describes the utility maximising balance between objectives and discretionary expenses.

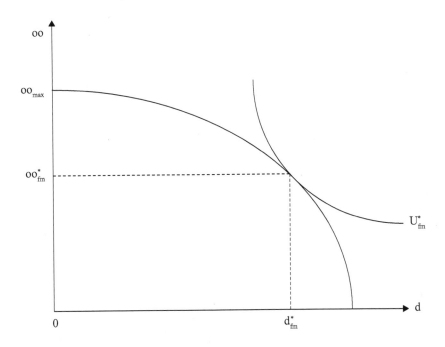

Figure 8.1 Utility maximizing founder-manager

Source: based on Jegers (2002: 434).

By definition, increasing discretionary expenses lowers the level of organisational objectives that can be reached, as resources are diverted from them. U^*_{fm} is the maximal utility that can be obtained by the founder-manager. The difference between oo_{max} and oo^*_{fm} depends on the shape of the indifference curve corresponding to U^*_{fm}. As there are no agency costs, and assuming there is no regulation on accounting and no external control, there is no need for accounting information aimed at mitigating agency costs. Clearly, this does not imply that there are no other reasons to justify the presence of accounting and control. The most obvious one is purely managerial: in order to manage the organisation in a rational way, accounting information is more than useful (Anthony 1989), and increasingly so when the organisation is larger, more complex, or more diversified.

The ineffective board

Though theoretically not very interesting, cases in which boards do not perform well in their monitoring tasks are widespread (see also Chapter 5). It would not be fair to assume that the manager, who is now hired by the board, is not interested at all in the organisational objectives (Chapter 5), but on average her preference for discretionary expenses will be relatively higher than for a founder-manager, making her indifference curves steeper. It can immediately be seen from Figure 8.1 that the organisational performance resulting from managerial utility maximisation (leading to a utility level U_{ib}^*)[6] will be lower than when having the founder managing the organisation, and the level of discretionary expenses higher: $oo_{fm}^* > oo_{ib}^*$ and $d_{fm}^* < d_{ib}^*$. The board being ineffective, it will not be able to impose accounting procedures in order to avoid agency costs, though managerial requirements might result in an accounting system being present.

The effective board

Reducing agency costs with accounting and financial control

If the board is maximally effective in observing the manager's behaviour, it has a direct way to incite her to pursue as much as possible the organisational objectives, allowing exactly the amount of discretionary expenses resulting in the managerial utility level to be equal to her reservation utility $U°$.

If managerial behaviour is not perfectly observable, the implementation of a system of accounting and financial control (assumed to be more elaborate than the one required for managerial purposes) results in a signal on the level of discretionary expenses. The additional resources required for this system can no longer be used for the pursuit of organisational objectives or for financing discretionary expenses, making the maximally obtainable level of organisational performance decrease to $oo_{max,acc}$ (Figure 8.2).

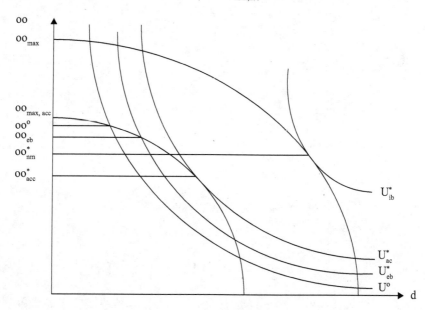

Figure 8.2 Accounting and control with an effective board

Source: based on Jegers (2002: 436-437).

---

6   'ib' stand for 'ineffective board'.

If there were no effect on managerial behaviour, managerial utility would now reach U^*_{acc}, and organisational performance oo^*_{acc}. A maximal impact on managerial behaviour would imply that her utility level would not exceed her reservation utility U°, with the concomitant performance level being oo°.[7] In reality, the effect of monitoring will be neither insignificant nor maximal. Assume managerial utility can be driven down to U^*_{eb} ($U^\circ < U^*_{eb} < U^*_{acc}$). If the resulting performance level oo_{eb} is higher than the performance level without monitoring (oo^*_{nm}, with managerial utility level U^*_{nm} ($= U^*_{ib}$)), it pays to have an accounting system, as the reduction of the maximal performance level does not prevent the performance level reached to increase. In the opposite case, accounting would increase the eventual agency cost incurred by the board.

Figure 8.2 allows us to hypothesise about the relationship between the dimension of the organisation and the presence of accounting and control systems. For larger organisations, the relative difference between oo_{max} and $oo_{max,acc}$ will be smaller. Therefore, the probability that oo_{eb} (performance with monitoring) exceeds oo^*_{nm} (performance without monitoring) increases, making the presence of accounting and control systems geared at monitoring management, *ceteris paribus*, more probable. As there are also operational reasons to expect larger organisations to have better developed accounting and control systems in place, it is difficult to determine from an empirical point of view whether the presence of these systems is dictated by operational needs or by the need to contain agency costs.

On the other hand, increasing complexity and diversification increase the cost of accounting and control, as illustrated in the paper by Beattie *et al.* (2001: 271), mentioned above, and therefore make the probability of oo_{eb} exceeding oo^*_{nm} smaller, contrary to the dimension effect. It is probable that efficiency effects dominate the relative inability to monitor management in a performance increasing way, meaning in terms of Figure 8.2 that without accounting oo_{max} would be rather small in complex and/or diversified organisations, perhaps even making it impossible for the manager to reach her reservation utility level.

Assuming the intensity of control is higher when performed by a 'Big' audit firm, indirect empirical proof of the relation between organisational dimension and intensity of audit is provided by Tate (2007).[8] Larger organisations on average were audited by an (at that time) Big Five auditor, whereas smaller ones were not (Tate 2007: 58). Furthermore, in the sample of Vermeer *et al.* (2007)[9] dimension (and the presence of a Big Four auditor) was positively related to the level of independence of the audit committee (Vermeer *et al.* 2007: 86), and the audit thoroughness that this can be assumed to imply.

---

7   Assuming the manager can be kept from choosing the lower performance-higher discretionary expenses combination resulting in the same utility.

8   15,955 US non-profit organisations for the period 1997-2002 receiving at least USD 300,000 in federal funds per year.

9   118 of the largest US non-profit organisations for 2004.

Refinements

In the previous section accounting and financial control were presented as constituting an indivisible whole carrying a given implementation cost decreasing oo_{max} to $oo_{max,acc}$ (Figure 8.2). In reality, a number of decisions can be considered in this context. There are at least three crucial decisions to be made. The first one is the choice between cash accounting and accruals accounting, the second one is to know whether financial information will be voluntarily disclosed, and the last one is a decision on hiring an external auditor. For each of these decisions a conceptual analysis comparable to the one of the previous section can be made (Jegers 2002), the bottom line always being the eventual level of organisational performance.

Turning to the choice between cash accounting and accruals accounting, 'in comparison with cash flow accounting, accruals adjustments demand a higher administrative and accounting cost' (Jones and Pendlebury 1996: 155). Introducing accruals accounting therefore can be justified only if it leads to stricter monitoring, more than compensating its higher cost in terms of reaching a higher level of organisational performance than under cash accounting. The paper by Calabrese (2011) is the only one directly looking at the non-profit organisation's choice between cash accounting and accruals accounting. In line with the size effect discussed in the previous section, he finds larger organisations[10] more frequently adopting an accruals based accounting system (Calabrese 2011: 82)[11] or switching to such a system (*ibid.*: 85).[12]

Christensen and Mohr (2003) observe a widely ranging diversity as to financial reporting and external control when looking at museums,[13] though a general attitude not to disclose financial information seems to prevail (Christensen and Mohr 2003: 148).

Donors as principals

When non-profit organisations are (partly) financed by (private or corporate) donors, the latter are a specific group of external stakeholders delegating decision authority to the organisations, and therefore principals, the organisation being the agent. Clearly, information asymmetries exist between the two, even more if there is no direct link between donors and eventual beneficiaries (Gordon and Khumawala 1999: 39). The question then is whether disclosing accounting information helps to reduce this gap, stimulating donors to be more generous than they would be in its absence.

Accounting here can be considered as a bonding cost from the point of view of the organisation, though '[t]here is limited empirical research examining

---

10   Size measured as the natural log of revenues. The results are robust to alternative specifications (*ibid.*: 86).
11   588,314 observations on 143,066 organisations not subject to federal audit requirements implying accrual basis accounting (US, 1998-2003).
12   205,506 observations on 71,351 organisations not subject to federal audit requirements implying accrual basis accounting (US, 1998-2003).
13   170 US museums in 1994.

the impact of *accounting* data on charitable giving decisions' (Parsons 2003: 104), an exception being Parsons (2007), who, using an experimental design on 8,022 fundraising appeals with and without financial information, found that existing donors 'are more likely to respond to a fundraising appeal if it includes positive [summarised] financial accounting information' (Parsons 2007: 190).

It also appears there is almost no research at all on the role of auditing, although audited financial statements are mentioned in the papers by Gordon and Khumawala (1999: 42) and Hyndman (1990), and Tate (2007: 58) establishes in her sample mentioned above that organisations audited by a Big Five audit firm rely more heavily on donations. An exception is the paper by Kitching (2009), who looks at the impact of choosing a Big 5 auditor versus another one.[14] Choosing a Big 5 auditor apparently conveys a signal on financial data reliability, irrespective of the possible impact of having appointed an auditor: donations are higher, and the impact of disclosed changes in donation price (see Chapter 7) is more pronounced (Kitching 2009: 519). A still unresolved issue is the question whether these effects compensate for the Big 5 premium, documented earlier in this chapter.

Accounting knowledge

In a profit context, it is taken for granted that both board members and managers fully understand the content and intricacies of accounting and financial statement analysis. In a non-profit setting, and especially in smaller organisations, this need not be the case. Frequently, both board members and staff are experts in the domains relevant for the organisation's mission, accounting knowledge not being a priority.[15] Therefore, accounting knowledge is a relevant issue in thinking about accounting in non-profit organisations.

The less qualified staff (or volunteers) responsible for implementing accounting procedures, the higher the impact on the implementation cost, negatively affecting $oo_{max,acc}$ in Figure 8.2, and therefore requiring a stronger impact on managerial discretionary behaviour to justify these procedures. Hence, from an agency point of view, the expectation that non-profit organisations will be less inclined than comparable profit organisations to implement these systems. Empirical results on this do not seem to be available, but Froelich *et al.* (2000) provide an indication that accounting knowledge considerations are relevant in non-profit organisations. About 50 interviews in large and medium sized US non-profit organisations revealed that 12 per cent of them did not have any accounting staff, whereas in about three-quarters of the remaining organisations nobody had an accounting education. In the same vein, Trigg and Nabangi (1995: 260) lament the deplorable quality of

---

14 228 US organisations soliciting funds nationally, being mandatorily audited, and not switching between Big 5-non Big 5 auditors (1,342 charity-year observations for 1995-2002).

15 See also the section earlier in this chapter on the attitude towards accounting and financial control.

financial statements issued by non-profit organisations: '[b]eggars cannot be choosy' (*ibid.*: 260), commenting on the staff or volunteers organisations (have to) use to comply with their accounting obligations. Also Keating *et al.* (2008) focus on accounting sophistication.[16] They relate misallocations of the costs of telemarketing campaigns to a lack of accounting knowledge, indirectly measured by total assets and the organisation's officers salaries and wages.

The same kind of reasoning can be applied to board members, leading to the expectation that the presence of accounting knowledge in the board makes it more probable that more sophisticated accounting systems will be instrumental in monitoring management (Christensen and Mohr 1995: 324; Miller-Millesen 2003: 524). Other principals to whom this line of thinking is applicable are the donors. Hyndman (1990: 300-306) indeed finds that they prefer summary financial information instead of the full financial statements.[17] As a matter of fact, he also finds that financial information is not considered to be that important when compared to reporting on operational activities. A comparable conclusion is reached by Buchheit and Parsons (2006) in their laboratory experiment.[18] Potential donors considered operational information combined with more general information on the organisation as significantly more useful than the general information alone, leading to a higher reported proclivity to donate, though this did not result in significantly more donations (Buchheit and Parsons 2006: 679). Only 37 per cent of the actual donors[19] were interested in making a financial comparison with a competing organisation when this information was made available in a very simple way. A total of 89 per cent of them eventually donated to the most efficient organisation, as measured by the percentage of total expenses dedicated to programme activities ($(C–A–f)/C$ where C stands for total costs, A for administrative costs excluding fundraising costs, and f for fundraising costs) (*ibid.*: 680). Summarising their results, they state that 'only a minority of individual donors request and use financial information, however ... there is a need for increased accuracy or not-for-profit expense classification' (*ibid.*: 667), reducing the scope for accounting manipulations, which are discussed at the end of this chapter.

The role of debt in explaining the presence of accounting and auditing

In the first writings on accounting theory for profit organisations there was already an important role for debt as it was assumed to (partly) contain agency problems between shareholders and management, though it is also acknowledged that it generates an additional agency conflict between shareholders (now acting as agents) and debtholders (the principals), which in

---

16 4,063 observations on 1,382 US nonprofit organisations (1999-2004) located in eight states.
17 Survey on a sample of 156 individual donors of the larger British charities.
18 157 undergraduate management accounting students.
19 Remember they were management accounting students.

its turn can be mitigated by imposing protective covenants, most of which will be expressed in accounting and auditing terms.

A comparable reasoning applies for non-profit organisations. Lenders to non-profit organisations know that these have specific objectives not expressed in financial terms, but as long as the organisation is expected to be able to pay interests and capital repayments when due, there is no reason to be financially worried.[20] To protect themselves, debtholders mostly require the borrowing organisation at least to periodically produce audited accounting information. Therefore, agency problems between board and management could be addressed in an indirect way by imposing the organisation to borrow, in order to have management forced not to divert earnings into discretionary expenses. Measuring potential agency costs in an organisation by dividing compensations, salaries and wages by total assets, Jegers (2011),[21] Jegers and Verschueren (2006)[22] and Verschueren and Jegers (2004),[23] find in a multivariate setting a positive correlation between these potential agency costs and the presence of debt, which is in line with an agency explanation of debt.

Accounting regulation and compliance

In the preceding sections it was assumed that non-profit organisations were not subject to any accounting regulation. This clearly is not the case, at least in most countries and for the larger organisations. Although other reasons to enact accounting regulations can be considered (Maijoor, 1991), accounting regulations for non-profit organisations are also easily understood in a principal–agent framework: authorities grant subsidies only under a number of conditions, making them the principal, and the organisation has to report on how the funds obtained have been used. Part of this reporting is financial reporting, which is therefore one of the monitoring instruments available to the authorities. The obligation for US hospitals to explicitly report charity care expenses from 1990 onwards can be interpreted in this vein as far as the non-profit hospitals are concerned (Eldenburg and Vines, 2004).

Accounting regulations make the interpretation of the submitted financial statements easier, enhancing the authority's chances of reducing residual losses, but also enabling other principals to interpret the statement's contents more correctly. Furthermore, uniform accounting rules reduce the monitoring costs as such, because of the possibility of common training programmes, and the availability of common rules that do not have to be reinvented at the organisational level. In the absence of governmental regulations, comparable (monitoring) cost advantages can be obtained by self-regulation, as witnessed in different US non-profit industries (Christensen and Mohr, 2003). In terms of Figure 8.2, this would imply that the difference between oo_{max} and $oo_{max, acc}$

20　See also Christensen and Mohr (1995: 324).
21　844 large Belgian non-profit organisations (2007).
22　22,766 Californian non-profit organisations (1999).
23　7,294 US cultural non-profit organisations (1999).

would be smaller as compared to a situation without common rules, making the usefulness of accounting and control more probable.

If the accounting regulations impose rules that imply at least an accounting intensity and sophistication required to cope with the board–management agency problems, there is no agency based need for additional accounting procedures. In the opposite case, where the rules to be applied due to regulation are not sufficient to optimally reduce agency costs between the board and management, one can expect accounting to be more elaborate than legally required.

The question whether to comply to accounting regulations is essentially an economic one. From the agent's point of view, not complying is optimal if the expected costs of noncompliance do not exceed the expected revenues brought about by misinforming the principal on the financial condition of the organisation, and possibly causing additional residual losses, especially in relationships where the authorities act as a principal.

Empirical research on compliance in non-profit organisations is scarce. Jegers and Houtman (1993) assess compliance by hospitals with accounting rules.[24] The compliance variable is the number of specific reporting violations of the law, of which the highest observable value possible was 32. There appeared to be no statistically significant difference in compliance behaviour between public and non-profit hospitals. Larger hospitals produced significantly better financial statements than smaller hospitals. This can be understood by noting that the relative cost of complying is smaller for larger hospitals (again making the difference between oo_{max} and $oo_{max, acc}$ in Figure 8.2 relatively smaller), combined with the expectation that the visibility of non-compliance (the 'political cost' as discussed below) and the ensuing negative impact on the manager's reputation is higher. In Calabrese's US sample referred to earlier, only 2 per cent of the financial statements of organisations subject to federal audit requirements, implying accrual basis accounting, did not report financial statements on an accrual basis. This percentage rises to 16 per cent in the case of state audit requirements (Calabrese 2011: 79). Krishnan and Schauer (2000) observe a comparatively low compliance for specific non-profit items.[25] Only 45 of the 164 organisations in the sample disclosed cash donations and pledges, and 91 disclosed donated materials and services. Also in this piece of research, larger organisations complied more. The authors also find an interesting effect of the auditor's reputation and dimension. After controlling for client characteristics (including size), compliance of organisations audited by one of the (at that time) Big Six is higher than that of organisations audited by large non-Big Six, which in turn is higher than that of organisations audited by small non-Big Six audit firms (Krishnan and Schauer 2000: 20). Which situation is optimal theoretically depends on the comparison between the value of the residual losses avoided and the additional audit fees (monitoring costs). Up to now, empirical work on this point does not seem to be available.

---

24   197 Belgian public and private non-profit hospitals in 1988.
25   Financial disclosures for 1994-1995 by 164 non-profit health and welfare organisations from Pennsylvania and New Jersey (US).

A different empirical paper on financial statement quality has been published by Yetman and Yetman (2004). These authors[26] compare at the state level basis the effect of governance mechanisms on accounting quality. They conclude that market governance (debt, donors) is more closely linked with high quality financial statements than regulatory governance (Yetman and Yetman 2004: 31). Apparently, at least for this sample, the cost of not complying is higher in the relationship with debtholders or donors as principals, than with regard to the regulatory authorities. This might explain the results obtained by Neely (2011), who finds no effect at all on financial reporting quality after the introduction of a Sarbanes-Oxley like legislation for non-profit organisations in California (US).[27] Thornton and Belski (2010) look at a market governance mechanism, and assess the impact of financial statement quality on donations.[28] This impact is clearly positive, illustrating the strength of market goverance. Furthermore, high quality financial statements lead to higher price-elasticities of donations, implying 'that donors can be more sensitive to variation in financial efficiency when they are more certain that financial information is accurate' (Thornton and Belski 2010: 2714). Note that when comparing with Yetman and Yetman (2004) causality is modelled in the reverse way. Controlling for endogeneity does not fundamentally alter their conclusions (Thornton and Belski 2010: 2709-2710).

Accounting choices

The empirical literature

Most accounting regulations, both for profit and non-profit organisations, allow for some choices to be made in a number of cases. Traditional examples are: depreciation rules (which frequently can be chosen out of a limited set of alternatives), stock valuation rules, capitalisation requirements. Theoretically, the eventual choice influences the information (or signal) given to the principal about the agent's financial performance, and therefore the agent might be induced to choose the most favourable alternative from her point of view (Steinberg 1993: 24). In a profit context, most choices are analysed with respect to their effect on managerial remuneration. But there is also published research available concluding that accounting choices in non-profit organisations can be understood.

The possible impact of accounting figures on remuneration schemes depends on the question 'whether charities explicitly use accounting measures

---

26   Between 6,168 and 15,669 yearly observations for the period 1985-2000 (US data).

27   The Californian Nonprofit Integrity Act was enacted in 2004. Data are on 2003 and 2005 (1,077 organisations). The Act only applies to organisations with gross revenues of at least USD 2 million, net of grants and public contract revenues. Therefore, smaller organisations were not included in the sample (Neely 2011: 108, 112). Financial reporting quality is proxied by three dummies: non-zero fundraising costs are reported when donations are received, professional fundraising fees are reported when professional fundraisers are contracted, and executive compensation is presented in a coherent way (*ibid.*, 114).

28   Unbalanced panel of 304,082 US organisations for 1998-2002.

for setting executive compensation' (Baber *et al.* 2002: 691). If not, from the revenue maximising manager's point of view, there is no point in purposely making any accounting choice. The paper closest to relevance in this context is written by Robbins *et al.* (1993).[29] The LIFO/FIFO choice and the depreciation method used are combined in a binary choice variable with two categories: income-increasing choices (84 per cent of the sample) and income-decreasing choices (16 per cent of the sample). Unfortunately, separate results for non-profit organisations are not given. In the sample as a whole, there seems to be a positive relation between the existence of management compensation plans and income-increasing choices, but this might be due to the presence of proprietary hospitals in the sample.

Chase and Coffman (1994) propose a 'political cost' reasoning to explain accounting choices by non-profit organisations. The reported wealth is assumed to impact on the government's and donors' willingness to provide subsidies and gifts. Higher levels of wealth are considered to be either a reason to reduce payments or a signal of financial viability entailing more subsidies and gifts, which are then expected not to be wasted. Apparently, the civil servants concerned and the public are assumed not to be able to assess the disclosed data correctly. On top of that, managers are believed to be concerned about their personal reputations, therefore trying to select accounting methods indicating maximal financial performance (return on endowments in this case). Chase and Coffman (1994)[30] consider the choice between fair market value reporting of the endowments and their reporting at cost. The results show that the institutions choosing the fair market value method are more endowed (supporting the financial viability reasoning) and realise higher returns on their endowments (not contradicting the reputation argument).

In Leone and Van Horn (2005), managerial reputation is again the focus, now in a traditional earnings management study. They find[31] data confirming the hypothesis that non-profit managers try to avoid losses, though they do not try to avoid negative earnings changes (Leone and Van Horn 2005: 835). As profit maximisation is not an objective of non-profit organisations, this result is not surprising: managerial reputation, then, is based on the fact that managers convey the message they do not endanger the financial viability of their organisations by accepting losses. A comparable study is described in Jegers (2010a).[32] He finds clear evidence of earnings manipulation towards zero. Further, potential agency conflicts[33] as well as the presence of debt induce earnings manipulation. Finally, larger organisations seem to be more inclined to manipulate, and, once they do, manipulate more to reach earnings levels closer to zero.

---

29   Survey on accounting choices in 298 US hospitals (public, private non-profit, and proprietary).
30   137 private colleges and universities in the US (data pertaining to 1989).
31   8,997 non-profit hospital-year observations (US, 1996-2002).
32   877 large Belgian non-profit organisations (2007).
33   Measured as salaries divided by total assets.

Very idiosyncratic earnings management incentives are provided by the UK National Health Service Trusts, which are subject to a statutory obligation to break even (Ballantine *et al.* 2007: 421), both profits and losses resulting in problems, losses being more severely punished than profits. In such a situation it does not come as a surprise that[34] earnings manipulating (through discretionary accruals) towards zero is observed (*ibid.*: 433-436), 'undermining' the reliability of financial accounting information (*ibid.*: 438).

Christensen and Mohr (1995) frame their accounting choice study on museums[35] explicitly in a principal–agent context. The choice here is whether or not to capitalise the museum's collection. There seems to be statistical support for political cost reasoning: the more federal government support is obtained, the less capitalisation is observed. The results of Eldenburg and Vines (2004) can also be understood in a principal–agent framework. They observe[36] that hospitals with higher cash levels are more prone to report a larger share of their uncompensated care as charity care, and not as bad debt, signalling to the (fiscal) authorities that their tax-exempt status is fully justified. As labelling uncompensated care as charity care implies forgoing any cash collection (e.g. through Medicare or Medicaid), hospitals with lower cash levels have to trade off the expected cost of losing their non-profit status with the expected cost of illiquidity.

Retrospective funding based on costs (Chapter 7) contains an incentive to choose accounting methods aimed at reporting costs as high as possible. This effect is of course not specific for non-profit organisations, but for all kinds of organisations that are financed in that way.

Finally, it is not only financial accounting choices that are possible. As will be shown below, cost accounting procedures and methods can be geared towards purposeful signalling.

Modelling earnings manipulations

As far as can be ascertained, Jegers (2010b) is the only paper containing a formal model of earnings manipulations in non-profit organisations. Both regular accounting choices and fraudulent registrations are considered to be manipulations, as both have similar effects on the earnings disclosed.

Two categories of manipulations can be considered: transactions can be rescheduled as to impact on recognition dates ('real manipulations', described by their effect on the earnings without manipulation Π by b_R), and purely administrative manipulations, without any real impact ('accounting manipulations': b_A). Both categories of manipulations entail real costs, such as manipulation time, or the impact of rescheduling if this causes the organisation's activities to be performed less efficiently. Therefore, the earnings disclosed can be written as:

---

34   859 English Trust-years (1999-2003).
35   1989 data on 106 US museums, of which 84 are non-profit.
36   98 non-profit hospitals located in Florida (1989–1991).

$$\Pi_M = \Pi + b_A + b_R - \text{real manipulation costs}$$

Note that the signs of b_A and b_R determine the direction in which earnings are changed: when positive, they make the disclosed earnings larger than the 'correct' earnings, and when negative, they make them smaller.

The organisation's utility function is the 'Steinbergian' one presented in Chapter 5:

$$U_{npo} = R + S + F - k\,(A + f)$$

where R represents all revenues except subsidies and funds raised, S is subsidies received, F is funds raised as the effect of fundraising costs f, A is administrative costs, and k ($0 \le k \le 1$) is, as before, the parameter reflecting the (lack of) similarity between the board's objectives and managerial objectives.[37] Contrary to the situation described in Chapter 5, both f and k are considered to be exogenously given, whereas (F+S) is a function of the earnings disclosed.[38]

Assuming the real manipulation costs to be quadratic in b_A and b_R, and also assuming the manager experiences personal disutility when manipulating, optimality conditions for b_A and b_R can be derived (Jegers 2010b: 412-413). Further, lower values of k (more agency costs) entail more manipulation, whatever the impact of the earnings disclosed on (F+S) (*ibid.*: 413). This is compatible with the results of Jegers (2010a) presented in the previous section.[39]

Financial statements of non-profit organisations

Content

Some authors contend that non-profit organisations' financial reports should 'reflect the service story of the entity instead of the net income or net loss' (Trigg and Nabangi 1995: 262), or at least should take account of the value of voluntary work (Mook *et al.* 2007: 60-61),[40] further bridging the informational gap between principal(s) and agent. Unfortunately for the adherents of this view, a financial statement is not an appropriate instrument to achieve this, as it is conceptually confined to the organisation's financial situation. Other sorts of reporting should be produced to describe the non-financial performance of the organisation (Falk 1992: 490), which is, without any doubt, far more important than its financial performance (Hyndman 1990: 304; Parsons 2003: 106), though the latter constrains the former to some extent. In that respect it is interesting to note that in a sample of museums,[41] 22 per cent of the annual

---

37 As before, k=0 reflects an organisation that is maximising the budget, whereas k=1 describes an organisation maximising service levels.

38 $\partial(F+S)/\partial\Pi_M > 0$ describing a form of crowding in, and $\partial(F+S)/\partial\Pi_M < 0$ describing a form of crowding out (see Chapter 7).

39 See especially Table 6, Panel A of Jegers (2010a).

40 They report 1 per cent of their sample described in the previous chapter doing this (*ibid.*: 63).

41 341 US museums, both public and non-profit (1994).

reports contained no financial data whatsoever, let alone a financial statement (Christensen and Mohr 2003).

Financial statement analysis

As far as financial analysis is concerned, there is no need to invent new concepts for non-profit organisations. Cash-flow, funds flow statement, profitability, liquidity, or financial structure ratios have the same interpretation as they have for profit organisations, though the operational implications of reaching certain values will be different, due to the differences in organisational goals (Abraham 2006). A dissenting view on the usefulness of profitability ratios for non-profit organisations is expressed by Wedig and Kwon (1995), who build on the old idea that accounting rates of return should reflect, in a direct or indirect way, internal rates of return earned on investments, which they do according to some, but not according to these authors (see e.g. Salamon (1985) and Fisher and McGowan (1983) respectively for seminal papers on both sides).

The only conceptual problem is the interpretation of the value added figure. For a profit organisation, its calculation and interpretation are founded on the assumption of perfectly competitive input and output markets, in which the unconstrained equilibriums between demand and supply reveal the societal value attached to the goods and services exchanged. The value added of a firm (as a component of (gross or net) national product) then is naturally defined as the difference between the value of the firm's output and the value of its input, values which can be estimated by using items in the financial statement of the firm. Adapting this calculation method for non-profit organisations is straightforward, but the value obtained is meaningless, as the conditions of perfectly competitive output and input markets are met only in a few cases. This is not to say that non-profit organisations do not generate societal value. The only point made here is that financial statement information will not help in determining this value.

Cost accounting in non-profit organisations

Cost accounting principles

As is the case for financial accounting techniques, cost accounting techniques are alike in profit organisations and non-profit organisations, as exemplified by most cost accounting textbooks (such as Horngren *et al.* 2005), which contain applications to both kinds of organisations.

As is well known, some arbitrariness cannot be avoided when allocating indirect costs to cost objects, allowing the possibility of window dressing if cost accounting data are to become known outside the organisation. Two situations can be considered: allocating indirect costs to profit activities and non-profit activities taking into consideration tax implications, and showing a high level of programme activities (as opposed to fundraising and administration)[42] when faced with potential donors.[43]

The cost of profit activities

Frequently, subsidising authorities calculate the amount to be granted taking into consideration the cost of the subsidised activities, especially when retrospective financing schemes are applied.[44] If organisations develop both subsidised and non-subsidised activities, it is rather difficult for the authorities to have a clear picture of the relevant costs. Cost accounting reduces this information asymmetry, especially in cases where cost accounting regulations are enacted to guide the allocation of the indirect costs. Sometimes these regulations are very strict and sometimes they give the organisations some leeway, in which case organisations could be inclined to allocate as much of the indirect costs as possible (and allowed, if they want to comply) to the subsidised activities. If the non-subsidised activities are taxed, for example to avoid less efficient non-profit organisations to enter profit markets (Sansing 1998), some trade-off has to be made between higher subsidies and lower taxes payable. Furthermore, if the non-subsidised activity is developed on a profit market, overhead allocation techniques potentially distort competition on this market (Weisbrod 1988: 116).

Both the papers by Cordes and Weisbrod (1998: 208)[45] and that by Yetman (2001: 308-309)[46] document cost shifting behaviour towards taxable activities, an opposite pattern not being apparent when looking at the allocated (aggregated) revenues (Yetman *et al.* 2009).[47] A number of organisations seem to be too zealous when shifting costs. In the US, more than half of the organisations reporting unrelated business income report not making profits on it, the aggregate value of losses exceeding that of profits (Sinitsyn and Weisbrod 2008: 164).[48] Remembering from Chapter 7 that profit activities by non-profit organisations are meant to generate profits, one can only hope that applying creative allocation rules is the explanation for this situation, and not engaging in unprofitable 'profit' activities. This is exactly inferred by Sinitsyn and Weisbrod (2008), who show[49] increased allocations of depreciation costs of assets jointly used for taxable and non-taxable activities to the taxable result

---

42   See also Chapter 7 on the price of donations.
43   For a theoretical analysis comparable to the one described earlier in this chapter with respect to earnings manipulations, see Jegers (2010b: 413-415).
44   See Chapter 7 and earlier in this chapter.
45   1,476 US non-profit organisations from the arts, education, health, and human services industries (data on 1992).
46   703 US non-profit organisations for 1995-1997 from the education, health, and charity industries.
47   1,612 US organisation-years for 1995-1997, also reported in Omer and Yetman (2003), where taxable incomes are also shown to cluster in a non-random way around zero.
48   Referring to work by Riley with IRS data up to 2002; see also Table 1 in Omer and Yetman (2003: 30) where total taxable expenses exceed total taxable revenues.
49   11,036 observations (1993-1997) on US non-profit organisations in six broad industries.

when there is a possibility to reduce taxes by doing so. They also observe that the choice of taxable activities is not random, but possibly guided by the presence of assets that can be jointly used.

Finally, note that cost shifting away from non-profit activities to profit activities reduces the reported cost of the former, which then appear to have been performed more efficiently.

Donors and organisational costs

In Chapter 7 and earlier in this chapter it was shown that there are reasons to believe that inefficiency measures or the price of donations, defined as[50]

$$\frac{F(1-t)}{C-A-f}$$

negatively affect the level of donations. Therefore, organisations have an incentive to guide indirect cost allocations in a way signalling high activity levels (Trussel 2003), especially when total programme costs (direct programme costs plus allocated indirect programme costs) are disclosed, together with the total administrative costs and the total fundraising costs. Krishnan *et al.* (2004) present empirical evidence of this. Comparing hospital data[51] in two databases that should contain the same information, they find that on average programme expenses reported in the publicly available database exceeded the same expenses reported in the other database with USD 13.9 million (Krishnan *et al.* 2004: 15). Furthermore, of the 95 hospitals reporting no fundraising expenses at all, at least 19 appear to have publicly documented fundraising activities (*ibid.*: 22),[52] apparently shifting the fundraising costs maximally to programme costs and/or administration costs. In their subsequent paper (Krishnan *et al.* 2006) they also find that the probability of not reporting any fundraising cost increases with the intensity of the relationship between donations and the share of programme costs in total costs. The same conclusion is reached when looking at the relationship between managerial remuneration and the share of programme costs. On the other hand, and contrary to the observations made in the case of the Avon Breast Cancer Walks (Tinkelman 2009), Bhattacharya and Tinkelman (2009: 485), applying visual inspection and statistical testing of ratio distributions, do not observe manipulations to reach watchdog standards on a programme activity ratio and a fundraising cost ratio,[53] though they

---

50   Where F is the amount of funds raised, t is the donor's (marginal) tax rate, C is total organisational costs, A is administrative costs net of fundraising costs, and f is fundraising costs.

51   719 hospital-year observations (Californian (US) non-profit hospitals, 1994–1998).

52   For a comparable result in which, in two samples, about 50 per cent of (respectively) more than 17,000 New York contribution receiving organisations and more than 16,000 US contribution receiving organisations (1992-1994) report fundraising expenses lower than 1 per cent of contributions, see Tinkelman (2006: 449).

53   111,894 US organisations for 2001.

acknowledge that this does not imply that there is no manipulation, as their sample consists only of organisations reporting non-zero administrative and fundraising costs. These organisations constitute only 24 per cent of the total population (Bhattacharya and Tinkelman 2009: 477). Finally, Keating *et al.* (2008) establish in their paper referred to earlier that misreporting the cost of telemarketing campaigns might lead to an underestimation of the fundraising share of total costs up to 15 per cent (*ibid.*: 445). The larger, more professional, and more intensely monitored organisations were found to be less misreporting, leading these authors to the suggestion that at least part of the misreporting can be explained by lack of accounting knowledge, deliberately manipulating not being the only possible explanatory factor.

Jones and Roberts (2006) do not look at programme activity share increasing manipulations, but at manipulations to dampen programme activity share variability. In their sample[54] they indeed find such behaviour. Two methods are used for this: influencing the absolute level of indirect costs, and adapting the allocation base.

Clearly, auditing cost accounting data will contribute to their reliability when disclosed (Tate 2007: 51), reducing information asymmetries between donors and the organisation.

---

54   708 organisation-year obervations of US non-profit organisations (1992-2000).

9 Financial management of non-profit organisations

Introduction

Leaving aside dividend decisions, which are not relevant because of the non-distribution constraint, the technicalities of non-profit financial management do not differ from those of traditional corporate finance, once differences in objectives are taken into account. This does not imply that a specific non-profit financial theory is not conceivable, though such a theory has not yet been formulated, except for some fragmented contributions to be discussed below. In a few early papers, such as Sloan *et al.* (1988) and Wedig (1994), attempts are made to apply standard financial theory to non-profit organisations, but these can be deemed conceptually flawed, as these theories' foundations (portfolio selection to arrive at an optimal risk-return combination for the investor, with ensuing systematic risk levels for the portfolio components and their required returns) are meaningless in a non-profit context because of the non-distribution constraint, which makes investments in (portfolios of) 'shares' of non-profit organisations not really a (financially) rational thing to do.

The topics discussed in this chapter are the non-profit specific sources of funds and their respective weights, the cost of non-profit capital, the capital structure of non-profit organisations, and the issue of financial vulnerability of non-profit organisations.

Sources of funds

Terminology

As is the case for profit organisations, we can distinguish two major categories of funds in non-profit organisations. Here we will call them equity or net assets on the one hand, and debt or liabilities on the other. The sum of the two equals the (accounting) value of all organisational assets (total assets), which is just another way of expressing the accounting equation. The relation between debt and equity is the organisation's capital structure.

Equity

Diversification of equity

Equity of non-profit organisations can be far more diversified than equity of profit organisations, as more sources can be tapped. Tuckman (1993) distinguishes two categories: internal sources and external sources. The former consist of contributions when founding the organisation (in cash or in kind), and profits/losses which have to be retained due to the non-distribution constraint, the latter of all kinds of donations, gifts and subsidies. Although all sources are not easily accessible for all sorts of non-profit organisations,[1] too much reliance on one might make the organisation vulnerable (Froelich 1999: 248, 253), both in a financial way (see below) and a functional way, when it has to face pressures to adapt organisational objectives ('goal displacement') or procedures. Too much diversification, on the other hand, possibly inflicts mutually exclusive obligations on the organisation.

Salamon and Anheier (1998: 219) present a comparative description of the most important categories of funds received by non-profit organisations in eight countries,[2] classified in eleven activity categories. They distinguish three sources of funds: privately paid fees (which indirectly add to equity, through the retained profit/loss of the organisation), subsidies, and private donations. Table 9.1 shows a wide variation between countries and industries. To give just one example, the main funds for social services are private payments in one of the countries in the sample, subsidies in six of these countries, and private donations in another one.

Table 9.1 Equity diversity in eight countries, by field (number of countries)

Field	Dominant funding by:		
	Private payments	*Subsidies*	*Private donations*
Culture, recreation	8	0	0
Education, research	4	4	0
Health	2	5	1
Social services	1	6	1
Environment	6	2	0
Development, housing	5	2	1
Civic, advocacy	4	4	0
Philanthropy	6	2	0
International	1	3	4
Business, professional	8	0	0
Other	3	0	1

Source: Salamon and Anheier (1998: 219).

---

1   And sometimes, as already mentioned in Chapter 7, not wanted.
2   France, Germany, Hungary, Italy, Japan, Sweden, UK, US.

Just looking at the predominant source of equity is a crude way of quantifying equity diversity. A more comprehensive measure is the diversity index (DI), which is based on the Herfindahl-Hirschman index of industrial concentration (n categories of equity Eq_i, with eq_i as the share of category i in total equity: $eq_i = Eq_i/\Sigma Eq_i$):

$$DI = \sum_{i=1}^{n} eq_i^2$$

When all equity categories increase, eq_i^2 can be substituted by $(\Delta Eq_i/\Sigma \Delta Eq_i)^2$, the squared share of the increase in equity category i within the total increase in equity. DI then reflects the diversity of additional equity. The usefulness of DI as diversification variable stems from its property to be negatively correlated with diversification, its range being $]0,1]$ (see Appendix X).

Chang and Tuckman (1994) empirically try to understand revenue diversification, the measurement of which is based on a variation on $\Delta Eq_i/\Sigma \Delta Eq_i$ when calculating DI.[3] They consider nine categories of revenues[4] (Chang and Tuckman 1994: 277). In a nutshell, they conclude that (*ibid.*: 281-284):

- the non-profit industry to which the organisation belongs affects the organisation's equity diversity;
- predominantly donative non-profit organisations are more diversified than predominantly commercial non-profit organisations, but the in-between organisations are even more diversified;[5]
- non-profit organisations reporting higher fundraising costs also have more diversified revenues.

Retaining earnings

As the non-distribution constraint does not imply that non-profit organisations are barred from making profits, the question arises whether it is better to accumulate profits (increasing equity) or to spend them in the pursuit of organisational objectives, eventually decreasing profits or even driving them to (less than) zero. Accumulating profits postpones some of the organisation's activities, and makes the organisation look wealthier, possibly inducing crowding out effects with respect to subsidies (Handy and Webb 2003) or donations.[6] Therefore, organisations accumulating profits must perceive some advantages from this, compensating for these obvious disadvantages.

Chang and Tuckman (1990: 123 ff) and Tuckman (1993: 208) discuss a number of these benefits: immediate availability (e.g. when confronted with

---

3   113,525 US non-profit organisations (data for 1986).
4   Donations, institutional charity, subsidies, programme revenues, membership dues, financial revenues from interests, dividends or rents, realised capital gains/losses, fundraising, other.
5   This last result can be partly induced by the way donative organisations and commercial organisations are defined, namely in terms of the share of respectively programme revenues and gifts and subsidies, which should exceed a threshold of 60 per cent.
6   See Chapter 7.

unexpected client needs), a lower need to justify later use, a safety net for harsh times,[7] less reliance on capital markets, and collecting funds for future expansions. Furthermore, there is no uncertainty as to the amount of funds available, which allows the organisation to use them in a straightforward way as collateral for debt. On top of that, the cost of retained earnings is lower than the cost of most alternatives (see below), at least when there are any alternatives. In general, one can say that retaining earnings in non-profit organisations mostly is the result of trading off current activities against (more) future activities.

Debt

Conceptually, debt of non-profit organisations is comparable to debt of profit organisations. Together with the spontaneous forms of debt,[8] all kinds of financial debt, including bonds, can also be observed.

A specificity for non-profit organisations is the fact that two groups of financial debt can be distinguished (Jegers 1997: 70): market debt and non-market debt. Market debt stems from loans granted by banks or other commercial lenders at market conditions, whereas non-market debt is provided by individuals[9] or institutions sympathetic to the organisation's mission. The financial cost of non-market debt, if any (Sloan *et al.* 1988), is lower than the cost of comparable market loans, as the lender's utility function contains more arguments than financial risk and financial returns. Therefore, a traditional risk-return portfolio approach to determine the cost of non-market debt is inappropriate, as the additional utility increasing factors compensating for lower return levels for a given risk level are not taken into consideration.

As far as market debt is concerned, its presence might give rise to agency problems between the organisation and its providers (Wedig *et al.* 1996: 1251), as the organisation could be inclined to give priority to organisational objectives over financial health, a situation the lender would like to avoid as much as possible, for example by negotiating protective covenants.[10]

In a number of countries, such as the US, systems exist by which interests paid to lenders to non-profit organisations are tax exempt. Whether a loan can be considered a market debt should then be assessed on an after-tax basis, notwithstanding the benefit for the borrowing organisation. It is not inconceivable that such tax exemptions engender effects that some would label perverse. Gentry (2002: 858-860)[11] finds convincing evidence of what he calls 'tax arbitrage': 'simultaneously borrowing in tax exempt markets and investing in non-operating assets (presumably with higher after-tax rates of return)' (Gentry 2002: 858).

---

7   See also Fisman and Hubbard (2003: 218).
8   Such as trade credit or tax (and other) accruals.
9   Possibly owners or members.
10   See also the section on the role of debt in explaining the presence of accounting and auditing (Chapter 7).
11   2,454 US non-profit hospitals (in 1995).

Cost of capital

Determining the cost of capital in a non-profit organisation

No doubt equity providers and non-market debt providers do not primarily require the organisation to generate financial surpluses, but expect the organisation's objectives to be aimed at (Ligon 1997: 68; Wedig 1994: 258), although they can also hope for prudent and rational financial management of the organisation's operations.

Together with the obvious financial requirements of the market lender, this puts some financial strain on the organisation's activities, in the sense that a minimal financial return on the funds invested might be necessary, not for the sake of profit maximisation, but for the sake of financial health and survival. This return is called the *cost of capital*, as it incorporates the financial returns expected by all the contributors of funds, be it equity or debt. Therefore, the organisation's activities and projects should (at least) generate a financial return equal to this cost of capital.

Technically, the cost of capital is the weighted average of the cost of equity and the cost of debt, the weights being equal to the value of equity and the value of debt[12] relative to the total value of the organisation. Theoretically, market values should be used, but these are not available in most circumstances. Therefore, departing from accounting figures is an accepted practice in empirical work. Further, from an economic point of view, a financial assessment of potential investments should be based on the marginal cost of capital, which is very difficult, if not impossible, to determine. Resorting to average values is a possible way out, though not always without validity problems.

In practice, measuring the cost of debt, both market debt and non-market debt, should not pose insurmountable problems.

This is not the case for the return on non-profit equity, for which no satisfying theory has been developed yet. An exception is found in the paper by Fama and Jensen (1985), who propose the donor's discount rate to play this role, based on a reasoning on the interaction between the need for funds and cost reductions (Fama and Jensen 1985: 116). This method has not gained wide acceptance, if any.

Some would argue that the required rate of return on non-profit equity ought to be zero, at least for donors who 'merely wish to have a brass plaque on a ... wall' (Sloan *et al.* 1988: 38),[13] or even negative if this allows the organisation to pursue its objectives, or the donor's objectives, in an effective way. On the other hand, as described above in the section on retained earnings, equity providers might have good reasons to require the organisation to generate a minimal return on equity. Logically, this return is lower than the expected cost of (non-market) debt, as otherwise the organisation would be better of, in terms of the activity levels that can be reached, not by raising additional

---

12   Taking into consideration the shares of market debt and non-market debt if both categories of debt are used.

13   See also Bowman (2002: 295).

equity, but by issuing (non-market) debt. Note that for profit organisations, risk considerations unequivocally lead to the required return of equity being higher that that on debt.

Investment analysis in non-profit organisations

Is there any empirical indication of non-profit managers using a required return criterion when making investment decisions? There is only one, rather old, empirical study on the matter (Kamath and Oberst 1992). They find[14] the average required rates of return presented in Table 9.2.

Table 9.2 Required rates of return in investment decisions (67 US hospitals, 1989)

	Required rate of return (%)
Public hospitals	8.19
Non religious non-profit hospitals	9.75
Religious hospitals	10.36
Profit hospitals	12.50

Source: Kamath and Oberst (1992: 210).

For this sample the required return of non-profit organisations is lower than the required return of profit organisations, which is at least compatible with the idea that the return required on equity is lower for the former than for the latter, and the fact that non-profit organisations can attract non-market debt, especially if it can be assumed that there need not be a substantial difference in the cost of market debt between the two institutional forms.

The same authors also note that about one-third of the sample still applied payback methods when evaluating investment proposals, instead of the theoretically correct present value based techniques (*ibid.*: 210-214).

Capital structure

The fact that for non-profit organisations the cost of equity is lower than the cost of debt implies that their most efficient capital structure would consist only of equity. But it is also 'a stylised fact that almost all NFP hospitals have debt obligations' (Wedig *et al.* 1988: 21). This statement is also valid for a large number of non-profit organisations in general: a little bit more than 50 per cent in the sample[15] of Jegers and Verschueren (2006) show any form of debt, and less then 20 per cent of their sample any financial debt (tax-exempt bonds, mortgages, and other notes payable) (Jegers and Verschueren 2006:

---

14   67 rather large US hospitals (1989).
15   22,766 Californian (US) non-profit organisations (1999).

320). These percentages are about 100 per cent and 67 per cent respectively in Jegers' (2011a) sample.[16] This begs the question how the presence of debt can be explained.

Bacon (1992)[17] and Bowman (2002)[18] assess the explanatory power of two classic profit organisation capital structure theories: the static trade-off theory[19] and the pecking order theory.[20] Their conclusions are divergent: Bacon (1992: 88) concludes that 'the pecking order hypothesis applies to [non-profit hospitals]' and that the '[s]tatic tradeoff ... does not seem to describe actual financing behaviour or [non-profit hospitals]' (*ibid.*: 89), whereas Bowman states that 'non-profit managers ... appear to use a static trade-off decision rule' (Bowman 2002: 308). There is probably no justification at all for framing the non-profit capital structure question into a traditional capital structure theory, as the objectives and incentives of the key players and organisations differ substantially from those involved in a profit environment.

A non-profit specific capital structure theory is presented by Jegers and Verschueren (2006: 312-314). They consider three groups of reasons explaining the presence and amount of debt in non-profit organisations.

A standard pecking order reasoning (Myers 1984) adapted to non-profit organisations would imply the following financing policy: avoid as much debt as possible in order to minimise the overall cost of capital, and resort to debt only when the equity available (donations, gifts, subsidies, retained earning, contributions) does not cover the organisation's financial needs. Following Gentry (2002: 846), such a case is labelled a situation in which *equity constraints* prevail.

A second group of reasons stems from potential agency problems.[21] Control rights enjoyed by managers enable them to extract rents. Mitigating the ensuing agency costs by designing incentive-based managerial remuneration contracts, a standard method in profit organisations, is less conceivable in non-profit organisations,[22] but issuing debt as an indirect way for the principals to monitor management might do the job (Jensen 1986). Repayment and interest obligations, and the concomitant screening by the lenders, can be assumed to curtail managerial discretion.

Non-profit organisations facing equity constraints do not automatically have access to (market or non-market) debt. For a variety of reasons some non-profit organisations are rightly or wrongly considered to be a 'good risk' by potential lenders, and other a 'bad risk'. Non-profit organisations unjustly considered bad risks are subject to *borrowing constraints* (Calem and Rizzo

---

16 844 large Belgian non-profit organisations (2007).
17 200 randomly chosen US non-profit general independent hospitals with more than 100 beds (1989 data).
18 1,393 US non-profit organisations (1991-1994).
19 Grounded by considering the investor's tax exemptions as an equivalent to the profit organisation's tax deductibility of interests.
20 Its idea is that the cheapest sources of funds will be tapped first.
21 See also Chapter 8.
22 See Chapter 5 on this.

1994). This story is the mirror image of the financing constraints reasoning developed for profit organisations in Fazzari *et al.* (1996).[23]

Jegers and Verschueren (2006) and Jegers (2011a) submit two questions to empirical testing in their samples described earlier in this chapter. How can the presence of debt be explained, and, for debt carrying organisations, how can the amount of debt be understood? A first conclusion is that in both samples the mechanism governing the decision to borrow differs from the mechanism determining the amount (relative to total assets) to be borrowed, once the decision to borrow has been made. Size, for example, has a significantly positive effect on the borrowing decision, but is negatively related to the amount borrowed.[24] The results concerning the three groups of reasons described above are mixed, possibly due to the proxies that had to be used. Equity constraints seem to exist as it comes to explain the level of debt. Potential agency problems seem to have a debt increasing effect.[25] As to borrowing constraints, they are only found in Jegers (2011a: 27) after having removed outliers.

Yan *et al.* (2009) wonder whether the organisation's revenue structure adds to our understanding of its capital structure. They conclude[26] that organisations showing more diversified revenue streams more easily take on long-term debt. There is no effect of revenue diversification on the level of debt. There also appears to be a positive effect of the shares of subsidies, donations, and operational revenues in total revenues on both the probability of indebtedness and the level of long term debts relative to total assets (Yan *et al.* 2009: 60).

Financial vulnerability

The least that can be expected from an organisation's financial management is that it aims at reducing its financial vulnerability, avoiding default payments and hence some form of bankruptcy or forced cessation of activities.

Though the use of the standard financial concepts as liquidity, profitability or financial leverage cannot be excluded in assessing an organisation's financial health,[27] Chang and Tuckman (1991: 659-662) propose, without any theoretical or empirical justification, four criteria to assess a non-profit organisation's financial vulnerability:

- capital structure, in accordance with traditional financial failure analysis: the more equity, the less vulnerable. The ratio they use in their descriptive

---

23 For a stylised corporate finance model, see Jegers (2011b). He finds that borrowing constraints are likely to arise when there are no substantial opportunities to increase revenues from fundraising and when non-profit managers are not willing to exert high fundraising efforts. Further, under these circumstances more agency problems lead to lower debt levels, contrary to situations without borrowing constraints, where more agency problems are shown to go together with higher debt levels.

24 See Jegers (2011a: 25, 27) for tables comparing the findings of both papers.

25 Except for the amount of financial debt in the sample of Jegers and Verschueren (2006).

26 3,840 observations on 1,387 US cultural organisations (2000-2003).

27 See also Chapter 8.

empirical work[28] is equity divided by revenues, but as this is the ratio of a stock variable and a flow variable, more standard capital structure ratios[29] relating two stock variables seem to be more appropriate;

- revenue diversification, which is discussed earlier in this chapter;
- the relative level of administrative costs. Their argument, which is open to dispute, is that high levels of administrative costs are relatively easy to cut back in times of financial hardship, without impacting on the organisation's activities;
- profitability, measured by the authors as operational profit/loss divided by revenues. The higher this ratio, the less vulnerable the organisation.

Hager (2001) assesses the predictive power of the four Chang-Tuckman vulnerability indicators.[30] Apart from a very few exceptions, these indicators are not at all mutually correlated (Hager 2001: 384). In a multivariate setting (*ibid.*: 387) the four indicators have the expected (and significant) effect on survival in the theatre subsample,[31] and three of them do so in the instrumental and choral music subsample,[32] the only exception being profitability, whose coefficient carries the expected sign, but is not significant. In the other subsamples[33] only a few significant coefficients are observed. Therefore, generally speaking, the predictive power of the model seems rather modest, even within the arts sectors (*ibid.*: 389). A comparable exercise is done by Trussel (2002),[34] defining financial vulnerability as a situation in which an equity decrease of at least 20 per cent is observed over 1997-1999.[35] Due to data limitations the administrative cost measure is not included, but size is added to the logit estimation. Controlling for industry, the three remaining Chang-Tuckman indicators perform as predicted, whereas there is also a significant positive effect of size on financial health (Trussel 2002: 25). For this study also, and despite the good performance of the explanatory variables, when predicting financial problems 'the error rates are still relatively high' (*ibid.*: 26). Keating *et al.* (2005)[36] use four different variables to measure financial vulnerability,[37] and reach comparable significance results, but also comparable explanatory power. Adding two independent variables to their model substantially increases its performance without making it more than modest. The variables are the share of commercial revenues (the more, the less vulnerable), and returns on endowments (the more, the less vulnerable).

---

28 4,370 US non-profit organisations for 1983 and 6,168 for 1985.
29 Such as equity/total assets or equity/debt.
30 7,266 US non-profit art organisations for 1990-1992, looking at their survival in 1994-1997.
31 2,043 observations.
32 2,483 observations.
33 Visual arts, museums, performing arts including schools and centres, dance organisations.
34 39,993 US non-profit organisations (data for 1996).
35 7,161 organisations being vulnerable according to this definition.
36 More than 280,000 US organisations (1998-2000).
37 Negative net assets, and a twenty five per cent decrease over one year of equity, revenues, and programme expenses respectively.

10 *Gaudium et spes*

Before the 1980s, non-profit organisations were absent in mainstream economic thinking, as illustrated by the statement by Hansmann (1986: 57) at that time, that 'the existing literature in ... economics ... has largely overlooked non-profit institutions', the reason being, also at that time, that 'economists usually view[ed] non-profits as economic anomalies, organisations outside the 'real' economic system' (Easly and O'Hara 1986: 85). Looking at the period starting in the 1980s, Steinberg (2004), in his introduction to the collection of the most important papers under the heading 'The economics of non-profit enterprises', sees three waves of academic research on the topic. The first deals with the non-profit organisation's objective function, the second with its role, and the third tries to integrate both. Concluding, he states that 'it is fair to say we now have a rudimentary understanding of the role and behavior of non-profit organisations within a broader economy' (Steinberg 2004: xxxviii). These aspects are the subject of the Chapters 3 to 5 of this book.

A comparison of the contents of the Steinberg volume with the contents of books on profit organisations carrying similar titles such as *Economics, Organisation and Management* (Milgrom and Roberts 1992) or *Managerial Economics and Organisation* (Acs and Grabowski 1996) reveals that the latter contain a substantial number of chapters on the economics of the internal functioning of firms, whereas the first only casually touches upon this topic (see also Chapter 1), a situation exactly reflecting the *status questionis* of both strands of research. This led us to state, also in 2004, that '... for internal functioning, economic theorists, and those disciplines that are heavily influenced by economic thought, have failed to explain the microeconomic internal functioning of NPOs.' (Helmig *et al.* 2004: 112). The Chapters 6-9 of this book show that this conclusion might have been too pessimistic, though most of the references therein are very recent. Furthermore, the sources from which they are drawn are very diverse and frequently outside the circle of the 'usual suspects' browsed by non-profit researchers. This might also explain the fact that these contributions do not always depart from the same conceptual framework, even when defining non-profit organisations, thus making comparison, let alone integration, difficult. Therefore, the Chapters 6-9 of this book can only be, at best, considered to be a first step towards some kind of integration of the managerial economic insights related to non-profit organisations' strategic management, marketing, accounting and finance, together with the human resources management aspects developed in Chapter 5 (remuneration, selection). This does not imply that everything has been said on the demand/supply aspects of non-profit organisations. As the Chapters 3-5 show, a lot of work remains to be done in this respect also.

Thought the title of this chapter has no connection with the pastoral document with the same title issued by the Roman Catholic Church after the Second Vatican Council, it perfectly reflects the actual situation of managerial economic research on non-profit organisations. We have enough reasons to be glad to have witnessed during the last two decades or so a growing body of high-quality research (*gaudium*), even though the parts of this body do not always seem to be connected with each other. The increasing rate by which this body grows, can only make us hope (*spes*) that it eventually will turn into a homogeneous and useful set of insights, of the same level, in all respects, as the level reached in the 'theory of the firm'. Given the role of non-profit organisations in society, this is something they deserve.

Appendix I   Further details of the international classification of non-profit organisations (ICNPO)

Group 1 Culture and recreation

1 100 Culture and arts

Media and communications. Production and dissemination of information and communication; includes radio and TV stations; publishing of books, journals, newspapers and newsletters; film production; and libraries.

Visual arts, architecture, ceramic art. Production, dissemination and display of visual arts and architecture; includes sculpture, photographic societies, painting, drawing, design centres and architectural associations.

Performing arts. Performing arts centres, companies and associations; includes theatre, dance, ballet, opera, orchestras, chorals and music ensembles.

Historical, literary and humanistic societies. Promotion and appreciation of the humanities, preservation of historical and cultural artifacts and commemoration of historical events; includes historical societies, poetry and literary societies, language associations, reading promotion, war memorials and commemorative funds and associations.

Museums. General and specialised museums covering art, history, sciences, technology and culture.

Zoos and aquariums.

1 200 Sports

Provision of amateur sport, training, physical fitness and sport competition services and events; includes fitness and wellness centres.

1 300 Other recreation and social clubs

Recreation and social clubs. Provision of recreational facilities and services to individuals and communities; includes playground associations, country clubs, men's and women's clubs, touring clubs and leisure clubs.

Service clubs. Membership organisations providing services to members and local communities, for example, Lions, Zonta International, Rotary Club and Kiwanis.

Group 2 Education and research

2 100 Primary and secondary education

Elementary, primary and secondary education. Education at elementary, primary and secondary levels; includes pre-school organisations other than day care.

2 200 Higher education

Higher education. Higher learning, providing academic degrees; includes universities, business management schools, law schools and medical schools.

2 300 Other education

Vocational/technical schools. Technical and vocational training specifically geared towards gaining employment; includes trade schools, paralegal training and secretarial schools.
Adult/continuing education. Institutions engaged in providing education and training in addition to the formal educational system; includes schools of continuing studies, correspondence schools, night schools and sponsored literacy and reading programmes.

2 400 Research

Medical research. Research in the medical field; includes research on specific diseases, disorders or medical disciplines.
Science and technology. Research in the physical and life sciences and engineering and technology.
Social sciences, policy studies. Research and analysis in the social sciences and policy area.

Group 3 Health

3 100 Hospitals and rehabilitation

Hospitals. Primarily inpatient medical care and treatment.
Rehabilitation. Inpatient health care and rehabilitative therapy to individuals suffering from physical impairments due to injury, genetic defect or disease and requiring extensive physiotherapy or similar forms of care.

3 200 Nursing homes

Nursing homes. Inpatient convalescent care and residential care, as well as primary health-care services; includes homes for the frail elderly and nursing homes for the severely handicapped.

3 300 Mental health and crisis intervention

Psychiatric hospitals. Inpatient care and treatment for the mentally ill.

Mental health treatment. Outpatient treatment for mentally ill patients; includes community mental health centres and halfway homes.

Crisis intervention. Outpatient services and counsel in acute mental health situations; includes suicide prevention and support to victims of assault and abuse.

3 400 Other health services

Public health and wellness education. Public health promotion and health education; includes sanitation screening for potential health hazards, first aid training and services and family planning services.

Health treatment, primarily outpatient. Organisations that provide primarily outpatient health services, e.g., health clinics and vaccination centres.

Rehabilitative medical services. Outpatient therapeutic care; includes nature cure centres, yoga clinics and physical therapy centres.

Emergency medical services. Services to persons in need of immediate care; includes ambulatory services and paramedical emergency care, shock/trauma programmes, lifeline programmes and ambulance services.

Group 4 Social services

4 100 Social services

Child welfare, child services and day care. Services to children, adoption services, child development centres, foster care; includes infant-care centres and nurseries.

Youth services and youth welfare. Services to youth; includes delinquency prevention services, teen pregnancy prevention, drop-out prevention, youth centres and clubs and job programmes for youth; includes YMCA, YWCA, Boy Scouts, Girl Scouts and Big Brothers/Big Sisters.

Family services. Services to families; includes family life/parent education, single parent agencies and services and family violence shelters and services.

Services for the handicapped. Services for the handicapped; includes homes, other than nursing homes, transport facilities, recreation and other specialised services.

Services for the elderly. Organisations providing geriatric care; includes in-home services, homemaker services, transport facilities, recreation, meal programmes and other services geared towards senior citizens (does not include residential nursing homes).

Self-help and other personal social services. Programmes and services for self-help and personal development; includes support groups, personal counselling and credit counselling/money management services.

4 200 Emergency and relief

Disaster/emergency prevention and control. Organisations that work to prevent, predict, control and alleviate the effects of disasters, to educate or otherwise prepare individuals to cope with the effects of disasters, or to provide relief to disaster victims; includes volunteer fire departments, life boat services etc.

Temporary shelters. Organisations providing temporary shelters to the homeless; includes travellers aid and temporary housing.

Refugee assistance. Organisations providing food, clothing, shelter and services to refugees and immigrants.

4 300 Income support and maintenance

Income support and maintenance. Organisations providing cash assistance and other forms of direct services to persons unable to maintain a livelihood.

Material assistance. Organisations providing food, clothing, transport and other forms of assistance; includes food banks and clothing distribution centres.

Group 5 Environment

5 100 Environment

Pollution abatement and control. Organisations that promote clean air, clean water, reducing and preventing noise pollution, radiation control, treatment of hazardous wastes and toxic substances, solid waste management and recycling programmes.

Natural resources conservation and protection. Conservation and preservation of natural resources, including land, water, energy and plant resources for the general use and enjoyment of the public.

Environmental beautification and open spaces. Botanical gardens, arboreta, horticultural programmes and landscape services; organisations promoting anti-litter campaigns; programmes to preserve the parks, green spaces and open spaces in urban or rural areas; and city and highway beautification programmes.

5 200 Animal protection

Animal protection and welfare. Animal protection and welfare services; includes animal shelters and humane societies.
Wildlife preservation and protection. Wildlife preservation and protection; includes sanctuaries and refuges.
Veterinary services. Animal hospitals and services providing care to farm and household animals and pets.

Group 6 Development and housing

6 100 Economic, social and community development

Community and neighbourhood organisations. Organisations working towards improving the quality of life within communities or neighbourhoods, e.g., squatters' associations, local development organisations and poor people's cooperatives.
Economic development. Programmes and services to improve economic infrastructure and capacity; includes building of infrastructure, such as roads, and financial services, such as credit and savings associations, entrepreneurial programmes, technical and managerial consulting and rural development assistance.
Social development. Organisations working towards improving the institutional infrastructure and capacity to alleviate social problems and to improve general public well-being.

6 200 Housing

Housing associations. Development, construction, management, leasing, financing and rehabilitation of housing.
Housing assistance. Organisations providing housing search, legal services and related assistance.

6 300 Employment and training

Job training programmes. Organisations providing and supporting apprenticeship programmes, internships, on the job training and other training programmes.
Vocational counselling and guidance. Vocational training and guidance, career counselling, testing and related services.
Vocational rehabilitation and sheltered workshops. Organisations that promote self-sufficiency and income generation through job training and employment.

Group 7 Law, advocacy and politics

7 100 Civic and advocacy organisations

Advocacy organisations. Organisations that protect the rights and promote the interests of specific groups of people, e.g., the physically handicapped, the elderly, children and women.

Civil rights associations. Organisations that work to protect or preserve individual civil liberties and human rights.

Ethnic associations. Organisations that promote the interests of or provide services to members belonging to a specific ethnic heritage.

Civic associations. Programmes and services to encourage and spread civic mindedness.

7 200 Law and legal services

Legal services. Legal services, advice and assistance in dispute resolution and court-related matters.

Crime prevention and public policy. Crime prevention to promote safety and precautionary measures among citizens.

Rehabilitation of offenders. Programmes and services to reintegrate offenders; includes halfway houses, probation and parole programmes, prison alternatives.

Victim support. Services, counsel and advice to victims of crime.

Consumer protection associations. Protection of consumer rights and the improvement of product control and quality.

7 300 Political organisations

Political parties and organisations. Activities and services to support the placing of particular candidates into political office; includes dissemination of information, public relations and political fund-raising.

Group 8 Philanthropic intermediaries and voluntarism promotion

8 100 Grant-making foundations

Grant-making foundations. Private foundations; including corporate foundations, community foundations and independent public-law foundations.

8 200 Other philanthropic intermediaries and voluntarism promotion

Volunteerism promotion and support. Organisations that recruit, train and place volunteers and promote volunteering.

Fund-raising organisations. Federated, collective fund-raising organisations; includes lotteries.

Group 9 International

9 100 International activities

Exchange/friendship/cultural programmes. Programmes and services designed to encourage mutual respect and friendship internationally.

Development assistance associations. Programmes and projects that promote social and economic development abroad.

International disaster and relief organisations. Organisations that collect, channel and provide aid to other countries during times of disaster or emergency.

International human rights and peace organisations. Organisations which promote and monitor human rights and peace internationally.

Group 10 Religion

10 100 Religious congregations and associations

Congregations. Churches, synagogues, temples, mosques, shrines, monasteries, seminaries and similar organisations promoting religious beliefs and administering religious services and rituals.

Associations of congregations. Associations and auxiliaries of religious congregations and organisations supporting and promoting religious beliefs, services and rituals.

Group 11 Business and professional associations, unions

11 100 Business associations

Business associations. Organisations that work to promote, regulate and safeguard the interests of special branches of business, e.g., manufacturers' association, farmers' association and bankers' association.

11 200 Professional associations

Professional associations. Organisations promoting, regulating and protecting professional interests, e.g., bar associations and medical associations.

11 300 Labour unions

Labour unions. Organisations that promote, protect and regulate the rights and interests of employees.

Source: United Nations (2003: Annex A1)

Appendix II Brooks-Ondrich (2007) method to determine the organisational objective function

To determine the first-order optimality conditions (assuming the second-order conditions are met), we derive the organisational utility function

$$U_{npo} = k_1(R+S+F(f,y)-f-A) + k_2(R+S+F(f,y)) + (1-k_1-k_2)((R+S+F(f,y)-f-A)/y)$$

with respect to the choice parameters f and y, which are assumed not be be influenced by each other (subscripts describing partial derivatives):

$$k_1(F_f-1) + k_2(F_f) + (1-k_1-k_2)((F_f-1)/y) = 0$$
$$k_1(R_y+F_y) + k_2(R_y+F_y)) + (1-k_1-k_2)((R_y+F_f)/y) - (1-k_1-k_2)((R+S+F(f,y)-f-A)/y^2) = 0$$

Inserting the three configurations of the k_i parameters described in the main text, leads directly to the conditions to be proved.

Appendix III · Proofs of an agent selection model, based on Besley and Ghatak (2005)

Part 1

First it is proved that at least one of the constraints should bind in an optimum. Suppose this is not the case: then, w_i can be reduced without violating the constraints,[1] simultaneously increasing the principal's utility. Therefore the original situation cannot be optimal.

Suppose now that the participation constraint binds, but not the subsistence constraint. In order not to violate the participation constraint, reducing w_i should be accompanied by an increase in b_i. Differentiating the binding participation constraint (after having substituted e_i by $b_i + \theta_i$) with respect to w_i results in the following condition for the change in b_i: $(b_i + \theta_i)db_i/dw_i = -1$. So, reducing w_i is feasible.

Substituting $e_i = b_i + \theta_i$ in the principal's maximand, differentiating with respect to w_i and then substituting $db_i/dw_i = -1/(b_i + \theta_i)$ results in an expression with a positive denominator and as numerator $b_i - \pi < 0$ (Besley and Ghatak 2005: 620, n11):

$$d[(\pi - b_i)\,(b_i + \theta_i) - w_i]/dw_i$$

$$= - db_i/dw_i\,(b_i + \theta_i - \pi + b_i) - 1$$

$$= (2b_i + \theta_i - \pi)/(b_i + \theta_i) - 1$$

$$= (b_i - \pi)/(b_i + \theta_i) < 0$$

Decreasing w_i then results in an increase in the principal's utility, which therefore could not have been optimal in the first place. Concluding, the subsistence constraint must bind.

---

1   e_i not being affected as $e_i = b_i + \theta_i$.

Part 2

The maximand now is $(\pi - b_i)(b_i + \theta_i) - w_{min}$ substituting $(b_i + \theta_i)$ for e_i. Deriving this with respect to b_i leads to the result in the main text.

Part 3

Substituting $b_i = (\pi - \theta_i)/2$ in $(\pi - b_i)(b_i + \theta_i) - w_{min}$ results in the expression described in the main text.

Appendix IV Derivation of the sustainable growth rate of a non-profit organisation (Jegers 2003)

Given the definitions of the variables in the main text, the return on assets can be written as

$$m = (Eq_1 - Eq_0)/TA_1$$

By definition, total assets can be expressed in the following way:

$$TA_1 = y_1/\alpha_1 = Eq_0 + (Eq_1 - Eq_0) + D_1$$

from which

$$SGR = \frac{y_1 - y_0}{y_0} = \frac{\alpha_1(Eq_0 + (Eq_1 - Eq_0) + D_1)}{y_0} - 1$$

Substituting y_0 by $\alpha_0 TA_0$, $(Eq_1 - Eq_0)$ by mTA_1, and Eq_t by D_t/d_t, results, after some tedious algebraic manipulations, in

$$SGR = \frac{(1+d_1)\alpha'}{(1+d_0)(1-(1+d_1)m)} - 1$$

Appendix V   Changes in demand and uncompensated care (Banks *et al.* 1997)

Part 1

We assume the following characterisations of the functions involved, using subscripts to describe partial derivatives:

$$P_y < 0 \qquad P_d > 0 \qquad (Py)_y < 0 \qquad V_y > 0$$

$$V_N > 0 \qquad V_{yy} > 0 \qquad V_{NN} > 0 \qquad V_{yN} > 0$$

The Lagrangian of the optimisation problem is

$$U_{np}(N) - \lambda(P(y; d).y - V(y,N) - F_x) = U_{np}(N) - \lambda\Pi$$

with the Lagrangian parameter λ.

With subscripts again describing partial derivatives, the first-order conditions for a maximum are:

$$U_{np,N} - \lambda\Pi_N = 0$$

$$\Pi_y = 0$$

$$\Pi = 0$$

These conditions have to be met whatever the value of d. Therefore

$$\Pi_d = 0 = P_y y_d y + P_d y + P y_d - V_y y_d - V_N N_d = (P_y y + P - V_y)y_d + P_d y - V_N N_d$$

As the expression in parentheses exactly equals Π_y, which is zero according to the second first-order condition, this can be written as

$$\Pi_y y_d + P_d y - V_N N_d = P_d y - V_N N_d$$

This being zero implies $N_d = P_d y / V_N$, which is positive as all the variables involved are positive. Therefore increasing demand goes together with increasing uncompensated care.

Part 2

Assume a profit hospital has to pay an amount L(N) to the authorities for not providing enough uncompensated care, with $L_N < 0$ and $L_{NN} < 0$. The hospital's profit therefore is

$$\Pi = P(y;d).y - V(y,N) - F_x - L(N)$$

Choosing y and N to maximise profits implies the following first-order conditions, with subscripts describing partial derivatives:

$$P_y y + P - V_y = 0$$

$$-V_N - L_N = 0$$

Both conditions have to be met whatever the value of d. Therefore

$$P_{yd} y + P_{yy} y_d y + P_y y_d + P_y y_d + P_d - V_{yy} y_d - V_{yN} N_d = 0$$

$$-V_{NN} N_d - V_{Ny} y_d - L_{NN} N_d = 0$$

This is a system of two linear equations in two unknowns (N_d and y_d) which can be solved applying Cramer's rule. For N_d the following expression can be derived:

$$N_d = \frac{\left(P_{yd} y + P_d\right) V_{Ny}}{V_{yN}^2 - (-L_{NN} - V_{NN})(P_{yy} y + 2P_y - V_{yy})}$$

As $\partial^2 \Pi / \partial y^2 = P_{yy} y + 2P_y - V_{yy}$, $\partial^2 \Pi / \partial N^2 = -V_{NN} - L_{NN}$, and $\partial^2 \Pi / \partial_y \partial_N = -V_{yN}$, the denominator is the opposite of the Hessian determinant of Π. Assuming again the second-order conditions to be met, the Hessian is negative definite, and its determinant positive. The denominator of N_d therefore is negative. As long as $P_{yd} > 0$ (the inverse demand curve getting flatter with increasing demand), the numerator is clearly positive. More generally, this is the case when $(P_{yd} y + P_d) > 0$, the expression in parentheses being the derivative of $P_d y$ with respect to y. This derivative being positive describes a situation in which, with increasing demand, sales increase more for higher values of y. Under this condition N_d is negative, implying the profit hospital decreases its provision of uncompensated care with increasing demand.

Appendix VI   A simplified version of Liu and Weinberg's (2004) model on non-profit/profit competition

Part 1

Deriving $\Pi_p = \frac{1}{2}(P_p - c_p)(1 - P_p + \theta P_{np}) = \frac{1}{2}(P_p - c_p - P_p^2 + c_p P_p + \theta P_p P_{np} - \theta c_p P_{np})$ with respect to P_p and setting this equal to zero leads to the result in the main text.

Part 2

Demand for the non-profit organisation is

$$q_{np} = \frac{1}{2}(1 - P_{np} + \theta P_p)$$

Given the optimal price for the profit organisation this can be written as

$$q_{np} = \frac{1}{2}(1 - P_{np} + \frac{1}{2}\theta(1 + \theta P_{np} + c_p)) = \frac{1}{2}(1 - (1 - \frac{1}{2}\theta^2)P_{np} + \frac{1}{2}\theta(1 + c_p))$$

From $\theta < 1$ we have $(1 - \frac{1}{2}\theta^2) > 0$, making q_{np} larger for smaller values of P_{np}. Given the zero profit constraint, the lowest possible value is c_{np}.

Part 3

In a duopoly with two identical profit organisations their optimal prices would be determined by the following reaction curves:

$$P_p^* = \frac{1}{2}(1 + \theta Pp^* + cp)$$

from which

$$P_p^* = (1 + c_p)/(2 - \theta)$$

We will prove that $(1 + c_p)/(2 - \theta) > \frac{1}{2}(1 + \theta c_p + c_p)$ $(\geq \frac{1}{2}(1 + \theta c_{np} + c_p))$. A necessary and sufficient condition for the first inequality to hold is $0 > c_p - 1 - \theta c_p$. As $c_p < 1$ this condition is always met.

Part 4

In a duoply with two profit organisations, their profits are

$$\frac{1}{2}\left(\frac{1+c_p}{2-\theta} - c_p\right)\left(1 - (1-\theta)\frac{1+c_p}{2-\theta}\right) \tag{VI.1}$$

The profit organisation's profit when competing a non-profit organisation is

$$\frac{1}{2}\left(\frac{1+\theta c_{np} + c_p}{2} - c_p\right)\left(1 - \frac{1 - \theta c_{np} + c_p}{2}\right) \tag{VI.2}$$

As proved in part 3 of this Appendix, the first bracketed factor of (VI.1) exceeds the first bracketed factor of (VI.2). This is also the case for the second bracketed factors, as a necessary and sufficient condition for this is $-2\theta - 2\theta c_p < -2\theta c_{np} - \theta + \theta^2 c_{np} - \theta c_p$. As $c_p < 1$ and $c_{np} \leq c_p$, this condition is always met, even when $c_{np} = c_p$. From (VI.2) it is also clear that decreasing c_{np} (and thus increasing the cost advantage to the non-profit organisation in the market) will decrease the profit organisation's profit even further, but only marginally. Compared to a situation with no cost differences, the difference affects only the profit organisation's profit in each factor of (VI.2) through $(c_{np} - c_p)\theta/2$.

Appendix VII   Wealth and voluntarily joining a board (based on Handy (1995))

In order to make the notation less cumbersome, the subscript 'b' will be dropped here, as this will not entail any notational ambiguity. Partial derivatives with respect to W will be denoted with an accent.

In this Appendix we will try to establish the sign of $\partial \hat{s}/\partial W$. As its denominator is a squared expression (different from zero), it is always positive. Therefore the sign of the numerator is also the sign of $\partial \hat{s}/\partial W$.

The numerator equals

$$(U^+ - U^-)(U^{\circ'} - U^{-'}) - (U^{+'} - U^{-'})(U^\circ - U^-)$$

As $\partial^2 U_b/\partial W \partial Rep < 0$, both $(U^{\circ'} - U^{-'})$ and $(U^{+'} - U^{-'})$ are negative, the last expression being larger in absolute value. If $\partial \hat{s}/\partial W$ were to be negative, the following condition should consequently prevail:

$$(U^+ - U^-)(U^{\circ'} - U^{-'}) < (U^{+'} - U^{-'})(U^\circ - U^-)$$

It is easy to see that the same condition must apply for $\partial \hat{s}/\partial W$ to be negative when reputation and wealth are complements ($\partial^2 U_b/\partial W \partial Rep > 0$).

Appendix VIII   Effect of different subsidy regimes on output and slack (Duizendstraal and Nentjes 1994)

Part 1: Lump sum subsidy

Substituting $S = S_{ls}$ and $C = C_d(y_d) + C_s(y_s)$ in the break even condition, taking into consideration that $C_s(y_s) = c_s y_s$, gives with a slightly simplified notation

$$S_{ls} + R = C_d + c_s y_s$$

from which $y_s(y_d)$ can be derived:

$$y_s = (S_{ls} + R - C_d)/c_s$$

Taking the first derivative with respect to y_d leads to the expression in the main text.

Part 2: Input subsidy

Substituting $S = sC$ and $C = C_d(y_d) + C_s(y_s)$ in the break even condition, taking into consideration that $C_s(y_s) = c_s y_s$, gives with a slightly simplified notation

$$s(C_d + c_s y_s) + R = C_d + c_s y_s$$

from which

$$y_s = (R - (1-s)C_d)/(1-s)c_s$$

Taking the first derivative with respect to y_d leads to the expression in the main text.

Part 3: (Desired) output subsidy

Substituting $S = gy_d$ and $C = C_d(y_d) + C_s(y_s)$ in the break even condition, taking into consideration that $C_s(y_s) = c_s y_s$, gives with a slightly simplified notation

$$gy_d + R = C_d + c_s y_s$$

from which

$$y_s = (gy_d + R - C_d)/c_s$$

Taking the first derivative with respect to y_d leads to the expression in the main text.

Part 4: Revenue based subsidy

Substituting $S = tR$ and $C = C_d(y_d) + C_s(y_s)$ in the break even condition, taking into consideration that $C_s(y_s) = c_s y_s$, gives with a slightly simplified notation

$$gy_d + R = C_d + c_s y_s$$

from which

$$y_s = ((1+t)R - C_d)/c_s$$

Taking the first derivative with respect to y_d leads to the expression in the main text.

Appendix IX   Profit activities by non-profit organisations (Schiff and Weisbrod 1991)

The Lagrangian of the optimisation problem is

$$U_{np}(y_d, y_c) - \lambda \, (F(y_d, y_c) + P_d y_d + P_c y_c - C(y_d, y_c))$$

with the Lagrangian parameter λ, from which we find the first-order optimality conditions:

$$\partial U_{np}/\partial y_d = \lambda(\partial F/\partial y_d + P_d - \partial C/\partial y_d) \qquad \text{(IX.1)}$$

$$\partial U_{np}/\partial y_c = \lambda \, (\partial F/\partial y_c + P_c - \partial C/\partial y_c) \qquad \text{(IX.2)}$$

λ is negative, as it measures the marginal utility of not breaking even anymore: not spending the whole budget available requires producing more of the commercial output (which generates funds, as shown below) and/or less of the desired output, reducing the organisation's utility.

In (IX.1), the left hand side is assumed to be positive. Therefore, the absolute value of $\partial C/\partial y_d$ should be larger than the marginal revenue of the desired output ($\partial F/\partial y_d + P_d$). As (IX.2) is assumed not te be positive, as is $\partial F/\partial y_c$, $P_c \geq - (\partial F/\partial y_c - \partial C/\partial y_c)$. Both conslusions lead to the statements in the main text.

Appendix X   Properties of the diversification index

The diversification index is defined as

$$DI = \sum_{i=1}^{n} eq_i^2$$

The eq_i are defined in such a way that $\Sigma eq_i = 1$.

If only one of the equity categories is different from zero, $DI = 1^2 = 1$.

If there are n (> 1) non zero equity categories, the following proves that $DI < 1$:

$$DI = \sum_{i=1}^{n} eq_i^2 < \left(\sum_{i=1}^{n} eq_i \right)^2 = 1$$

Suppose the number of non zero-equity categories is given (n). Intuitively, a situation in which each category takes the same share is more diversified than a less equal distribution. In such a situation, DI, given n, will be minimal. To prove this, we solve

$$\min_{eq_1, \ldots, eq_n} \sum_{i=1}^{n} eq_i^2$$

$$\text{s.t. } \Sigma eq_i = 1$$

The Langrangian of this problem is, with λ as the Langrangian multiplier:

$$\sum_{i=1}^{n} eq_i^2 - \lambda (\Sigma eq_i - 1)$$

The n first-order conditions read for all i:

$$2eq_i - \lambda = 0$$

from which $eq_1 = eq_2 = \ldots = eq_n = 1/n$. The DI value corresponding with this situation is

$$DI = \Sigma(1/n)^2 = n(1/n)^2 = 1/n$$

Therefore, when there are n (> 1) equity categories, $1/n \leq DI < 1$, and if n grows to infinity, the lower bound of DI goes to zero.

Bibliography

Abdul-Rahman A.R. and Goddard A. (1998) 'An interpretative inquiry of accounting practices in religious organisations: Emerging theoretical perspectives', *Financial Accountability and Management*, 14: 183–201.

Abraham A. (2006) 'Financial management in the non-profit sector: A mission-based approach to ratio analysis in membership organisations', *Journal of American Academy of Business*, 10: 212-217

Acs Z.J. and Gerlowski D.A. (1996) *Managerial economics and organisation*, New Jersey: Prentice Hall.

Alchian A.A. and Demsetz H. (1972) 'Production, information costs and economic organisation', *American Economic Review*, 62: 777-795.

Alexander J.A. and Lee S.-Y. D. (2006) 'Does governance matter? Board configuration and performance in not-for-profit hospitals', *Milbank Quarterly*, 84: 733-758.

Amirkhanyian A.A., Kim H.J. and Lambright K.T. (2008) 'Does the public sector outperform the non-profit and for-profit sectors? Evidence from a national panel study on nursing home quality and access', *Journal of Policy Analysis and Management*, 27: 329-353.

Andreasen A.R. (2009) 'Cross-sector marketing alliances. Partnerships, sponsorships, and cause-related marketing', in Cordes, J.J. and Steuerle, C.E. (eds) *Non-profits & business*, Washington DC: The Urban Institute Press.

Andreoni J. (1990) 'Impure altruism and donations to public goods: A theory of warm-glow giving', *Economic Journal*, 100: 464-477.

Andreoni J. and Payne A.A. (2003) 'Do government grants to private charities crowd out giving or fund-raising?', *American Economic Review*, 93: 792-812.

— (2011) 'Is crowding out due entirely to fundraising? Evidence from a panel of charities', *Journal of Public Economics*, 95: 334-343.

Anheier, H.K. (1995) 'Theories of the non-profit sector: Three issues', *Non-profit and Voluntary Sector Quarterly*, 24: 15-23.

— (2005) *Non-profit organisations: Theory, management, policy*, London: Routledge.

Anheier H.K. and Ben-Ner A. (1997) 'Economic theories of non-profit organisations: A Voluntas symposium', *Voluntas: International Journal of Voluntary and Non-profit Organisations*, 8: 93-96.

Anheier H.K. and Salamon L.M. (2006) 'The non-profit sector in comparative perspective', in Powell W.W. and Steinberg R. (eds.) *The non-profit sector: A research handbook*, 2nd edition, New Haven: Yale University Press.

Ansoff H.I. (1965) *Corporate strategy: An analytic approach to business policy for growth and expansion*, New York: McGraw Hill.

Anthony R.N. (1980) 'Making sense of nonbusiness accounting', *Harvard Business Review*, 58: 83-93.

— (1989) *Should business and nonbusiness accounting be different?* Boston: HBS Press.

Apinunmahakul A., Barham V. and Devlin R.A. (2009) 'Charitable giving, volunteering, and the paid labor market', *Non-profit and Voluntary Sector Quarterly*, 38: 77-94.

Aralumpalam W. and Stoneman P. (1995) 'An investigation into the givings by large corporate donors to UK charities, 1979-86', *Applied Economics*, 27: 935-945.

Arrow K.J. (1963) 'Uncertainty and the welfare economics of medical care', *American Economic Review*, 53: 941-973.

Austin J.E. (2000) 'Strategic collaboration between non-profits and businesses', *Non-profit and Voluntary Sector Quarterly*, 29 (Supplement): 69-97.

Baber W.R., Daniel P.L. and Roberts A.A. (2002) 'Compensation to managers of charitable organisations: An empirical study of the role of accounting measures of program activities', *Accounting Review*, 77: 679-693.

Bacon P.W. (1992) 'Do capital structure theories apply to non-profit hospitals?', *Journal of the Midwest Finance Association*, 21: 86-90.

Badelt C. (1997) 'Entrepreneurship theories of the non-profit sector', *Voluntas: International Journal of Voluntary and Non-profit Organisations*, 8: 162-178.

Bakija J. and Heim B. (2008) 'How does charitable giving respond to incentives and income? Dynamic panel estimates accounting for predictable changes in taxation', NBER Working Paper 14237, Washington DC: NBER.

Ballantine J., Forker J. and Wendel J. (2007) 'Earnings management in English NHS Hospital Trusts', *Financial Accountability and Management*, 23: 421-440.

Ballou J.P. (2005) 'An examination of the presence of ownership effects in mixed markets', *Journal of Law, Economics and Organisations*, 21: 228-255.

Ballou J.P. and Weisbrod B.A. (2003) 'Managerial rewards and the behaviour of for-profit, governmental, and non-profit organisations: Evidence from the hospital industry', *Journal of Public Economics*, 87: 1895-1920.

Banks D.A., Paterson M. and Wendel J. (1997) 'Uncompensated hospital care: Charitable mission or profitable business decision?', *Health Economics*, 6: 133-134.

Barbetta G.P., Turati G. and Zago A.M. (2007) 'Behavioral differences between public and private not-for-profit hospitals in the Italian national health service', *Health Economics*, 16: 75-96.

Bauer K. (2009) 'Conflicts of interest on the board of directors of non-profit hospitals: theory and evidence', *Annals of Public and Cooperative Economics*, 80: 469-497.

Baum J.A. and Oliver C. (1996) 'Toward an institutional ecology of organisational founding', *Academy of Management Journal*, 39: 1378-1427.

Baumol W.J. (1959) *Business behavior, value and growth*, New York: Harcourt, Brace, Wald (1967 reprint).

Beattie V., Goodacre A., Pratt K. and Stevenson J. (2001) 'The determinants of audit fees-evidence from the voluntary sector', *Accounting and Business Research*, 31: 243-274.

Beckmann M.J. (1988) 'Managers as principals and agents', in Bamberg G. and Spremann K. (eds.) *Agency theory, information, and incentives*, Berlin: Springer Verlag.

Ben-Ner A. (2002) 'The shifting boundaries of the mixed economy and the future of the non-profit sector', *Annals of Public and Cooperative Economics*, 73: 5-40.

Ben-Ner A. and Van Hoomissen T. (1991) 'Non-profit organisations in the mixed economy: A demand and supply analysis', *Annals of Public and Cooperative Economics*, 6: 519-550.

Bennett R. and Savani S. (2003) 'Predicting the accuracy of public perceptions of charity performance', *Journal of Targeting, Measurement and Analysis for Marketing*, 11: 329-342.

Benz M. (2005) 'Not for the profit, but for the satisfaction? Evidence on worker well-being in non-profit firms', *Kyklos*, 58: 155-176.

Besley T. and Ghatak M. (2005) 'Competition and incentives with motivated agents', *American Economic Review*, 95: 616-636.

Bhattacharya R. and Tinkelman D. (2009) 'How tough are Better Business Bureau/Wise Giving Alliance financial standards?', *Non-profit and Voluntary Sector Quarterly*, 38: 467-489.

Bilodeau M. and Slivinski A. (1996) 'Volunteering non-profit entrepreneurial services', *Journal of Economic Behavior and Organisation*, 31: 117-127.

— (1997) 'Rival charities', *Journal of Public Economics*, 66: 449-467.

— (1998) 'Rational non-profit entrepreneurship', *Journal of Economics and Management Strategy*, 7: 221-571.

Bises B. (2000) 'Exemption or taxation for profits of non-profits? An answer from a model incorporating managerial discretion', *Public Choice*, 104: 19-39.

Bolton P. and Mehran H. (2006) 'An introduction to the governance and taxation of not-for-profit organisations', *Journal of Accounting and Economics*, 41: 293-305.

Boraas S. (2003) 'Volunteerism in the United States', *Monthly Labor Review*, 126: 3-11.

Borgonovi F. (2006) 'Do public grants to American theatres crowd-out private donations?', *Public Choice*, 126: 429-451.

Boris E.T. and Steuerle C.E. (2006) 'Scope and dimension of the non-profit sector', in Powell W.W. and Steinberg R. (eds.) *The non-profit sector: A research handbook*, 2nd edition, New Haven: Yale University Press.

Borjas G.J., Frech H.E. and Ginsburg P.B. (1983) 'Property rights and wages: The case of nursing homes', *Journal of Human Resources*, 17: 231-246.

Borzaga C. and Tortia E. (2006) 'Worker motivation, job satisfaction, and loyalty in public and non-profit social services', *Non-profit and Voluntary Sector Quarterly*, 35: 225-248.

Bowman W. (2002) 'The uniqueness of non-profit finance and the decision to borrow', *Non-profit Management and Leadership*, 12: 293-311.

— (2009) 'The economic value of volunteers to non-profit organisations', *Non-profit Management and Leadership*, 19: 491-506.

Brandl J. and Güttel W.H. (2007) 'Organisational antecedents of pay-for-performance systems in non-profit organisations', *Voluntas: International Journal of Voluntary and Non-profit Organisations*, 18: 176-199.

Brickley J.A. and Van Horn R.L. (2002) 'Managerial incentives in non-profit organisations: Evidence from hospitals', *Journal of Law and Economics*, 45: 227-249.

Brickley J.A., Van Horn R.L. and Wedig G.J. (2010) 'Board composition and non-profit conduct: evidence from hospitals', *Journal of Economic Behavior and Organisation*, 76: 196-208.

Brody E. (1996) 'Agents without principals: The economic convergence of the non-profit and for-profit organisational forms', *New York Law School Law Review*, 40: 457-536.

Brooks A.C. (2005) 'What do non-profit organisations seek? (And why should policymakers care?)', *Journal of Policy Analysis and Management*, 24: 543-558.

— (2007) 'Income tax policy and charitable giving', *Journal of Policy Analysis and Management*, 26: 599-612.

Brooks A.C. and Ondrich J.I. (2007) 'Quality, service level, or empire: Which is the objective of the non-profit art firm?', *Journal of Cultural Economics*, 31: 129-142.

Brown E. and Slivinski A. (2006) 'Non-profit organisations and the market', in Powell W.W. and Steinberg R. (eds.) *The non-profit sector: A research handbook*, 2nd edition, New Haven: Yale University Press.

Brown W.A. (2005) 'Exploring the association between board and organisational performance in non-profit organisations', *Non-profit Management and Leadership*, 15: 317-339.

Brown W.O., Helland E. and Smith J.K. (2006) 'Corporate philanthropic practices', *Journal of Corporate Finance*, 12: 855-877.

Bryson J.M. (1991) *Strategic planning for public and non-profit organisations*, San Francisco: Jossey-Bass.

Buchheit S. and Parsons L.M. (2006) 'An experimental investigation of accounting information's influence on the individual giving process', *Journal of Accounting and Public Policy*, 25: 666-686.

Buelens A., Pepermans R., Flion I. and Mentens C. (1999) 'Differences in motivation to manage between the profit and non-profit sector', in Pepermans R., Flion I., Ardts J.C., Jansen P.G. (eds.) *Managerial behaviour: Empirical studies on management development and socialiation*, Leuven: Acco.

Burik D. and Duvall T.J. (1985) 'Hospital cost accounting: Strategic considerations', *Healthcare Financial Management*, 15: 19-28.

Caers R., Du Bois C., Jegers M., De Gieter S., De Cooman R. and Pepermans R. (2005a) 'Selecting the 'best' employee for the job: An agency-stewardship view on applicant selection in non-profit organisations', paper presented at the 5th European Institute for Advanced Studies in Management Workshop on the Challenges of Managing the Third Sector, Belfast.

— (2005b) 'Recruiting non-profit employees: An agency-stewardship theory on motivational differences and selective contracting', paper presented at the European Conference of the ISTR and EMES, Paris.

— (2006a) 'A micro-economic perspective on manager selection in non-profit organisations', paper presented at the European Academy of Management (EURAM) Conference, Oslo. A revised version is forthcoming in the *European Journal of Operational Research*.

Caers R., Du Bois C., Jegers M., De Gieter S., Schepers C. and Pepermans R. (2006b) 'Principal-agent relationships on the stewardship-agency axis', *Non-profit Management and Leadership*, 17: 25-47.

Calabrese T.D. (2011) 'Public mandates, market monitoring, and non-profit financial disclosures', *Journal of Accounting and Public Policy*, 30: 71-88.

Calem P.S. and Rizzo J.A. (1994) 'Financing constraints and investment: New evidence from hospital industry data', Federal Reserve Bank of Philadelphia – Economic Research Division, Working Paper FRB-ERD WP 94-9.

Callen J.R. (1994) 'Money donations, volunteering and organisational efficiency', *Journal of Productivity Analysis*, 5: 215-228.

Callen J.R. and Falk H. (1993) 'Agency and efficiency in non-profit organisations: The case of "specific health focus" charities', *Accounting Review*, 68: 48-65.

Callen J.L., Klein A. and Tinkelman D. (2003) 'Board composition, committees, and organisational efficiency: The case of non-profits', *Non-profit and Voluntary Sector Quarterly*, 32: 493-520.

Canning D., Jefferson C.W. and Spencer J.E. (2003) 'Optimal credit rationing in not-for-profit financial institutions', *International Economic Review*, 44: 243-261.

Cardinaels E. (2009) 'Governance in non-for-profit hospitals: effects of board members' remuneration and expertise on CEO compensation', *Health Policy*, 93: 64-75.

Carey K. (1994) 'Cost allocation patterns between hospital impatient and outpatient departments', *Health Services Research*, 29: 275-292.

Carroll R. and Joulfaian D. (2005) 'Taxes and corporate giving to charity', *Public Finance Review*, 33: 300-317.

Castaneda M.A. and Falschetti D. (2008) 'Does hospital's profit status affect its operational scope?', *Review of Industrial Economics*, 33: 129-159.

Castaneda M.A., Garen J. and Thornton J. (2008) 'Competition, contractibility, and the market for donors to non-profits', *Journal of Law, Economics, and Organisations*, 24: 215-246.

Chambré S.M. and Fatt N. (2002) 'Non-profit organisations in an emerging policy domain', *Non-profit and Voluntary Sector Quarterly*, 34: 502-524.

Chang C.F. and Tuckman H.P. (1990) 'Why do non-profit managers accumulate surpluses, and how much do they accumulate?', *Non-profit Management and Leadership*, 1: 117-135.

— (1991) 'Financial vulnerability and attrition as measures of non-profit performance', *Annals of Public and Corperative Economics*, 62: 655-672.

— (1994) 'Revenue diversification among non-profits', *Voluntas: International Journal of Voluntary and Non-profit Organisations*, 5: 273-290.

— (1996) 'The goods produced by non-profit organisations', *Public Finance Quarterly*, 24: 25-43.

Chase B.W. and Coffman E.N. (1994) 'Choice of accounting method by non-for-profit institutions: Accounting for investments by colleges and universities', *Journal of Accounting and Economics*, 18: 233-243.

Chau N.H. and Huysentruyt M. (2006) 'Non-profits and public good provision: A contest based on compromises', *European Economic Review*, 50: 1909-1935.

Chen G. (2009) 'Does meeting standards affect charitable giving? An empirical study of New York Metropolitan Area charities', *Non-profit Management and Leadership*, 19: 349-365.

Chesteen S., Helgheim B., Randall T. and Wardell D. (2005) 'Comparing quality of care in non-profit and for-profit nursing homes: A process perspective', *Journal of Operations Management*, 23: 229-242.

Chillemi O. and Gui B. (1991) 'Uninformed customers and non-profit organisation: Modelling "contract failure" theory', *Economics Letters*, 35: 5-8.

Chinman M.J. and Wandersman A. (1999) 'The benefits and costs of volunteering in community organisations: Review and practical implications', *Non-profit and Voluntary Sector Quarterly*, 28: 46-64.

Chou S.-Y. (2002) 'Asymmetric information, ownership and quality of care: An empirical analysis of nursing homes', *Journal of Health Economics*, 21: 293-311.

Christensen A.L. and Mohr R.M. (1995) 'Testing a positive theory model of museum accounting practices', *Financial Accountability and Management*, 11: 317-335.

— (2003) 'Not-for-profit annual reports: What do museum managers communicate?, *Financial Accountability and Management*, 19: 139-158.

Clark R.C. (1980) 'Does the non-profit form fit the hospital industry?', *Harvard Law Review*, 93: 1417-1489.

Cleveland G. and Krashinsky M. (2009) 'The non-profit advantage: producing quality in thick and thin child care markets', *Journal of Policy Analysis and Management*, 28: 440-462.

Coase R. (1937) 'The nature of the firm', *Economica*, 4: 386-405.

Cordes J.J. and Weisbrod B.A. (1998) 'Differential taxation of non-profits and the commercialisation of non-profit revenues', *Journal of Policy Analysis and Management*, 17: 195-214.

Courtney R. (2002) *Strategic management for voluntary non-profit organsations*, London: Routledge.

David G. (2009) 'The convergence between for-profit and non-profit hospitals in the United States', *International Journal of Health Care Finance and Economics*, 9: 403-428.

Davis K. (1972) 'Economic theories of behavior in non-profit private hospitals', *Economic Business Bulletin*, 24: 1-13.

De Andrés-Alonso P., Azofra-Palenzuela V. and Romero-Merino M.E. (2010) 'Beyond the disciplinary role of governance : how boards add value to Spanish foundations', *British Journal of Management*, 21: 100-114.

De Andrés-Alonso P., Martín Cruz N. and Romero-Merino M.E. (2006) 'The governance of non-profit organisations: Empirical evidence from nongovernmental development organisations in Spain', *Non-profit and Voluntary Sector Quarterly*, 35: 588-604.

De Cooman R., De Gieter S., Pepermans R., Du Bois C., Caers R. and Jegers M. (2007) 'Graduated teacher's motivation for choosing a job in education', *International Journal of Educational and Vocational Guidance*, 7: 123-136.

De Gieter S., De Cooman R., Pepermans R., Caers R., Du Bois C. and Jegers M. (2006) 'Dimensionality of the Pay Satisfaction Questionnaire: A validation study in Belgium', *Psychological Reports*, 98: 640-650.

Desmet P. (1998) 'The impact of mail order on subsequent donations: An experiment', *Financial Accountability and Management*, 14: 203-215.

Dewaelheyns N., Eecklo K., Van Herck G., Van Hulle C. and Vleugels A. (2009) 'Do non-profit nursing homes separate governance roles? The impact of size and ownership characteristics', *Health Policy*, 90: 188-195.

DiMaggio P. (1987) 'Non-profit organisations in the production and distribution of culture', in Powell W.W. (ed.) *The non-profit sector: A research handbook*, New Haven: Yale University Press.

Dollery B.E. and Wallis J.L. (2003) *The political economy of the voluntary sector*, Cheltenham: Edward Elgar.

Dolnicar S. and Randle M. (2007) 'What motivates which volunteers? Psychographic heterogeneity among volunteers in Australia', *Voluntas: International Journal of Voluntary and Non-profit Organisations*, 18: 135-155.

Douglas J. (1987) 'Political theories of non-profit organisations', in Powell W.W. (ed.) *The non-profit sector: A research handbook*, New Haven: Yale University Press.

Drummond M.F., Stoddart G.L. and Torrance G.W. (1987) *Methods for the economic evaluation of health care programmes*, Oxford; Oxford University Press.

Du Bois C., Caers R., Jegers M., De Cooman R., De Gieter S. and Pepermans R. (2005) 'The link between composition and preferences of the board: An empirical analysis for non-profit school boards', paper presented at the 5th European Institute for Advanced Studies in Management Workshop on the Challenges of Managing the Third Sector, Belfast.

— (2006) 'Agency problems between board and manager: A discrete choice experiment in Flemish non-profit schools', Paper presented at the European Academy of Management (EURAM) Conference, Oslo.

Du Bois C., Caers R., Jegers M., Schepers C., De Gieter S. and Pepermans R. (2004a) 'Objectives of non-profit organisations: A "managerial economics" perspective', *Zeitschrift für öffentliche und gemeinwirtschaftliche Unternehmen (Journal for Public and Non-profit Services)*, 27: 288-302.

— (2004b) 'Agency problems and unrelated business income: An empirical analysis', *Applied Economics*, 36: 2317-2326.

Duggan M. (2002) 'Hospital market structure and the behavior of not-for-profit hospitals', *Rand Journal of Economics,* 33: 433-446.

Duizendstraal A. and Nentjes A. (1994) 'Organisational slack in subsidised non-profit institutions', *Public Choice*, 81: 297-321.

Duncan J.B., Flesher D.L. and Stocks, M.H. (1999) 'Internal control systems in US churches: An examination of the effects of church size and denomination on systems of internal control', *Accounting, Auditing and Accountability Journal*, 12: 142–163.

Dyl E.A., Frant H.L. and Stephenson C.A. (2000) 'Governance and funds allocations in United States medical research charities', *Financial Accountability and Management,* 16: 335-352.

Easley D. and O'Hara M. (1983) 'The economic role of the non-profit firm', *Bell Journal of Economics,* 4: 531-538.

— (1986) 'Optimal non-profit firms', in Rose-Ackerman S. (ed.) *The economics of non-profit organisations,* New York: J. Wiley.

— (1988) 'Contracts and asymmetric information in the theory of the firm', *Journal of Economic Behavior and Organisation,* 9: 229-246.

Eldenburg L. and Kallapur S. (1997) 'Changes in hospital service mix and cost allocations in response to changes in Medicare reimbursement schemes', *Journal of Accounting and Economics,* 23: 31-51.

Eldenburg L., Hermalin B.E., Weisbach M.S. and Woskinska M. (2000) 'Hospital governance, performance objectives, and organisational form', Working Paper.

— (2004) 'Hospital governance, performance objectives, and organisational form: Evidence from hospitals', *Journal of Corporate Finance,* 10: 527-548.

Eldenburg L. and Soderstrom N. (1996) 'Accounting system management by hospitals operating in a changing regulatory environment', *Accounting Review,* 71: 23-42.

Eldenburg L. and Vines C.C. (2004) 'Non-profit classification decisions in response to a change in accounting rules', *Journal of Accounting and Public Policy,* 23:1–22.

Enjolras B. (2002) 'Does the commercialisation of voluntary organisations 'crowd out' voluntary work?' *Annals of Public and Cooperative Economics,* 73: 375-398.

Erus B. and Weisbrod B.A. (2003) 'Objective functions and compensation structures in non-profit and for-profit organisations: Evidence from the 'mixed' hospital industry', in Glaeser E.L. (ed.) *The governance of not-for-profit firms,* Chicago: University of Chicago Press.

Falk H. (1992) 'Towards a framework for not-for-profit accounting', *Contemporary Accounting Research,* 8: 468–499.

Fama E.F. and Jensen M.C. (1983a) 'Separation of ownership and control', *Journal of Law and Economics,* 26: 301-325.

— (1983b) 'Agency problems and residual claims', *Journal of Law and Economics,* 26: 327-349.

— (1985) 'Organisational forms and investment decision', *Journal of Financial Economics,* 14: 101-119.

Farsi M. and Filippini M. (2004) 'An empirical analysis of cost efficiency in non-profit and public nursing homes', *Annals of Public and Cooperative Economics,* 75: 339-365.

Fazzari S.M., Hubbard R.G. and Petersen B.C. (1996) 'Financing constraints and corporate investments: Response to Kaplan and Zingales', NBER Working Paper 5462.

Feigenbaum S. (1987) 'Competition and performance in the non-profit sector: The case of US medical research charities', *Journal of Industrial Economics,* 35: 241-253.

Feiock R.C. and Jang H.S. (2009) 'Non-profits as local government service contractors', *Public Administration Review,* 64: 668-680.

Fisher F.M. and McGowan J.J. (1983) 'On the misuse of accounting rates of return to infer monopoly profits', *American Economic Review,* 73: 82-97.

Fisman R. and Hubbard R.G. (2003) 'The role of non-profit endowments', in Glaeser E.L. (ed.) *The governance of not-for-profit firms*, Chicago: University of Chicago Press.

Foster V., Mourato S., Pearce D. and Özdemiroğlu E. (2001) *The price of virtue*, Cheltenham: Edward Elgar.

Francois P. (2001) 'Employee care and the role of non-profit organisations', *Journal of Institutional and Theoretical Economics*, 157: 443-464.

Frank R.G. and Salkever D.S. (1991) 'The supply of charity services by non-profit hospitals: Motives and market structure', *Rand Journal of Economics*, 22: 430-445.

Frey B.S. (1997) 'On the relationship between intrinsic and extrinsic work motivation', *International Journal of Industrial Organisation*, 15: 427-439.

Frey B.S. and Götte L. (1999) 'Does pay motivate volunteers?' University of Zurich, Working Paper ISSN 1424-0459.

Frey B.S. and Jegen R. (2001) 'Motivation crowding theory', *Journal of Economic Surveys*, 15: 589-611.

Froelich K.A. (1999) 'Diversification of revenue strategies: Evolving resource dependence in non-profit organisations', *Non-profit and Voluntary Sector Quarterly*, 28: 246-268.

Froelich K.A., Knoepfle T.W. and Pollak T.H. (2000) 'Financial measures in non-profit organisation research in comparing IRS 990 Return and audited financial statement data', *Non-profit and Voluntary Sector Quarterly*, 29: 232-254.

Galaskiewicz J., Bielefeld W. and Dowell M. (2006) 'Networks and organisational growth: A study of community based non-profits', *Administrative Science Quarterly*, 51: 337-380.

Galaskiewicz J. and Sinclair Colman M. (2006) 'Collaboration between corporations and non-profit organisations', in Powell W.W. and Steinberg R. (eds.) *The non-profit sector: A research handbook*, 2nd edition, New Haven: Yale University Press.

Garcia I. and Marcuello C. (2002) 'Family model of contributions to non-profit organisations and labour supply', *Applied Economics*, 34: 259-265.

Gassler R.S. (1997) 'The economics of the non-profit motive: Formulation of objectives and constraints for firms and non-profit enterprises', *Journal of Interdisciplinary Economics*, 8: 265-280.

Gazley B. and Brudney J.L. (2007) 'The purpose (and perils) of government-non-profit partnership', *Non-profit and Voluntary Sector Quarterly*, 36: 389-415.

Gentry W.M. (2002) 'Debt, investment and endowment accumulation: The case of not-for-profit hospitals', *Journal of Health Economics*, 21: 845-872.

Gertler P. and Kuan J. (2009) 'Does it matter who your buyer is? The role of non-profit mission in the market for corporate control of hospitals', *Journal of Law and Economics*, 52: 295-306.

Gill M., Flynn R.J. and Reissing E. (2005) 'The Governance Self-Assesment Checklist: An instrument for assessing board effectiveness', *Non-profit Management and Leadership*, 15: 271-294.

Glaeser E.L. (2003) 'Introduction', in Glaeser E.L. (ed.) *The governance of not-for-profit firms*, Chicago: University of Chicago Press.

Glaeser E.L. and Shleifer A. (1998) 'Not-for-profit entrepreneurs', NBER Working Paper 6810.

— (2001) 'Not-for-profit entrepreneurs', *Journal of Public Economics*, 81: 99-115.

Gordon T.P. and Khumawala S.B. (1999) 'The demand for not-for-profit financial statements: A model of individual giving', *Journal of Accounting Literature*, 18: 31–56.

Gordon T.P., Knock C.L. and Neely D.G. (2009) 'The role of rating agencies in the market for charitable contributions: an empirical test', *Journal of Accounting and Public Policy,* 28: 469-484.

Grabowski D.C. and Hirth R.A. (2003) 'Competitive spillovers across non-profit and for-profit nursing homes', *Journal of Health Economics*, 22: 1-22.

Grimalda G. and Sacconi L. (2005) 'The constitution of the not-for-profit organisation: Reciprocal conformity to morality', *Constitutional Political Economy*, 16: 249-276.

Gui B. (1991) 'The economic rationale for the "third sector": Non-profit and other noncapitalist organisations', *Annals of Public and Cooperative Economics*, 62: 551-572.

Guo B. (2006) 'Charity for profit? Exploring factors associated with the commercialisation of human service non-profits', *Non-profit and Voluntary Sector Quarterly*, 35: 123-138.

Hager M.A. (2001) 'Financial vulnerability among arts organisations: A test of the Tuckman-Chang measures', *Non-profit and Voluntary Sector Quarterly*, 30: 376-392.

Hager M., Rooney P. and Pollak T. (2002) 'How fundraising is carried out in US non-profit organisations', *International Journal of Non-profit and Voluntary Sector Marketing*, 7: 311-324.

Haider A. and Schneider U. (2010) 'The influence of volunteers, donations and public subsidies on the wage level of non-profit workers: evidence from Austrian matched data', *Annals of Public and Cooperative Economics*, 81: 1-20.

Hall P.D. (2006) 'A historical overview of philanthropy, voluntary associations, and non-profit organisations in the United States, 1600-2000', in Powell W.W. and Steinberg R. (eds.) *The non-profit sector: A research handbook*, 2nd edition, New Haven: Yale University Press.

Hallock K.F. (2002) 'Managerial pay and governance in American non-profits', *Industrial Relations*, 41: 377-406.

Handy F. (1995) 'Reputation as collateral: An economic analysis of the role of trustees of non-profits', *Non-profit and Voluntary Sector Quarterly*, 24: 293-305.

— (1997) 'Coexistence of non-profit, for-profit and public sector institutions', *Annals of Public and Cooperative Economics*, 68: 201-223.

Handy F., Cnaan R.A., Brudney J.L., Ascoli U., Meijs L.C. and Ranade S. (2000) 'Public perception of "Who is a volunteer": An examination of the net-cost approach from a cross-cultural perspective', *Voluntas: International Journal of Voluntary and Non-profit Organisations*, 11: 45-65.

Handy F. and Katz E. (1998) 'The wage differential between non-profit institutions and corporations: Getting more by paying less?' *Journal of Comparative Economics*, 26: 246-261.

Handy F., Mook L. and Quarter J. (2008) 'The interchangeability of paid staff and volunteers in non-profit organisations', *Non-profit and Voluntary Sector Quarterly*, 37: 76-92.

Handy F. and Srinivasan N. (2004) 'Valuing volunteers: An economic evaluation of the net benefits of hospital volunteers', *Non-profit and Voluntary Sector Quarterly*, 33: 28-54.

Handy F. and Webb N.J. (2003) 'A theoretical model of the effects of public funding on saving decisions by charitable non-profit service providers', *Annals of Public and Cooperative Economics*, 74: 261-282.

Hansmann H.B. (1980) 'The role of non-profit enterprise', *Yale Law Journal*, 89: 835-901, partly reprinted on pages 57-84 of Rose-Ackerman S. (ed.) (1986) *The economics of non-profit organisations*, New York: J. Wiley.

— (1986) 'The role of non-profit enterprises', in Rose-Ackerman S. (ed.) *The economics of non-profit organisations*, New York: J. Wiley.

— (1987) 'Economic theories of non-profit organisation', in Powell W.W. (ed.) *The non-profit sector: A research handbook*, New Haven: Yale University Press.

Hansmann H., Kessler D. and McClellan M. (2003) 'Ownership form and trapped capital in the hospital industry', in Glaeser E.L. (ed.) *The governance of not-for-profit firms*, Chicago: University of Chicago Press.

Harrison T.D. (2008) 'Taxes and agglomeration economies: how are they related to non-profit firm location?', *Southern Economic Journal*, 75: 538-557.

Havens J.J., O'Herlihy M.A. and Schervish P.G. (2006) 'Charitable giving: How much, by whom, to what, and how?', in Powell W.W. and Steinberg R. (eds.) *The non-profit sector: A research handbook*, 2nd edition, New Haven: Yale University Press.

Helmig B., Jegers M. and Lapsley I. (2004) 'Challenges in managing non-profit organisations: A research overview', *Voluntas: International Journal of Voluntary and Non-profit Organisations* 15: 101-116.

Herman R.D. (2005) 'Board members of non-profit organisations as volunteers', in Brudney J.L. (ed.) *Emerging areas of volunteering*, Indianapolis: ARNOVA.

Herman R.D. and Heimovics R.D. (1990) 'The effective nonprofict executive leader of the board', *Non-profit Management of Leadership*, 1: 167-180.

— (1991) *Executive leadership in non-profit organisations: New strategies for shaping executive-board dynamics*, San Franciso: Jossey-Bass.

Herman R.D. and Renz D.O. (2004) 'Doing things right: Effectiveness in local non-profit organisations, a panel study', *Public Administration Review*, 64: 694-204.

Heutel G. (2009) 'Crowding out and crowding in of private donations and government grants', NBER Working Paper 15004, Washington DC: NBER.

Hewitt J.A. and Brown D.K. (2000) 'Agency costs in environmental not-for-profits', *Public Choice*, 103: 168-183.

Heyes A. (2005) 'The economics of vocation or 'why is a badly paid nurse a good nurse'?', *Journal of Health Economics*, 24: 561-569.

Hirth R.A. (1999) 'Consumer information and competition between non-profit and for-profit nursing homes', *Journal of Health Economics*, 18: 219-240.

Holtmann A.G. (1983) 'A theory of non-profit firms', *Economica*, 50: 439-449.

Holtmann A.G. and Ullmann S.G. (1991) 'Transaction costs, uncertainty, and not-for-profit organisations: The case of nursing homes', *Annals of Public and Cooperative Economics*, 62: 641-654.

Horne C.S., Johnson J.L. and Van Slyke D.M. (2005) 'Do charitable donors know enough – and care enough – about government subsidies to affect private giving to non-profit organisations?', *Non-profit and Voluntary Sector Quarterly*, 34: 136-149.

Horngren C.T., Bhimani A., Datar S.M. and Foster G. (2005) *Management and cost accounting*, 3rd edition, Harlow: Prentice Hall – Pearson Education.

Horwitz J.R. and Nichols A. (2009) 'Hospital ownership and medical services: market mix, spillover effects, and non-profit objectives', *Journal of Health Ecomics*, 28: 924-937.

Hustinx L. (2005) 'Weakening organisational ties? A classification of styles of volunteering in the Flemish Red Cross', *Social Service Review*, 79: 624-652.

Hwang H. and Powell W.W. (2009) 'The rationalisation of charity: The influences of professionalism in the non-profit sector', *Administrative Science Quarterly*, 52: 268-298.

Hyndman N. (1990) 'Charity accounting – an empirical study of the information needs of contributors to UK fund raising charities', *Financial Accountability and Management*, 6: 295-307.

Inglis S. and Cleave S. (2006) 'A scale to assess board member motivations in non-profit organisations', *Non-profit Management and Leadership*, 17: 67-80.

Iyer, V.M. and Watkins, A.L. (2008) 'Adaption of Sarbanes-Oxley measures by non-profit organisation: an empirical study', *Accounting Horizons*, 22: 255-277.

Jackson A.C. and Donovan F. (1999) *Managing to survive: Manageral practice in not-for-profit organisations*, Buckingham: Open University Press.

Jacobs F.A. and Marudas N.P. (2009) 'The combined effect of donation price and administrative inefficiency on donations to US non-profit organisations', *Financial Accountability and Management*, 25: 33-53.

James R.N. and Sharpe D.L. (2007) 'The nature and causes of the U-shaped charitable giving profile', *Non-profit and Voluntary Sector Quarterly*, 36: 218-238.

Jegers M. (1997) 'Portfolio theory and non-profit financial stability: A comment and extension', *Non-profit and Voluntary Sector Quarterly*, 26: 65-72.

— (2002) 'The economics of non profit accounting and auditing: Suggestions for a research agenda', *Annals of Public and Cooperative Economics*, 73: 429-451.

— (2003) 'The sustainable growth rate of non-profit organisations: The effect of efficiency, profitability and capital structure', *Financial Accountability and Management*, 19: 309-313.

— (2010a) 'Do non-profit organisations manipulate earnings? An empirical study', Paper presented at the 33th European Accounting Association Congress, Istanbul.

— (2010b) 'The effect of board-manager agency conflicts on non-profit organisations' earnings and cost allocation manipulations', *Accounting and Business Research*, 40: 407-419.

— (2011a) 'On the capital structure of non-profit organisations: a replication and extension with Belgian data', *Financial Accountability and Management*, 27: 18-31.

— (2011b) 'Financing constraints in non-profit organisations: a 'Tirolean' approach', *Journal of Corporate Finance*, 17: 640-648.

Jegers M. and Houtman C. (1993) 'Accounting theory and compliance to accounting regulations: The case of hospitals', *Financial Accountability and Management*, 9: 267-278.

Jegers M., Kesteloot K., De Graeve D. and Gilles W. (2002) 'A typology for provider payment systems in health care', *Health Policy*, 60: 255-273.

Jegers M. and Verschueren I. (2006) 'On the capital structure of non-profit organisations: An empirical study for Californian organisations', *Financial Accountability and Management*, 22: 309-329.

Jensen M.C. (1986) 'Agency costs of free cash flow, corporate finance, and takeovers', *American Economic Review*, 76: 323-329.

Jensen M.C. and Meckling W.H. (1976) 'Theory of the firm: Managerial behavior, agency costs and ownership structure', *Journal of Financial Economics*, 3: 305-360.

Jobome G.O. (2006) 'Management pay, governance and performance: The case of large UK non-profits', *Financial Accountability and Management*, 22: 331-358.

Jones C.L. and Roberts A.A. (2006) 'Management of financial information in charitable organisations: The case of joint-cost allocations', *Accounting Review*, 81: 159-178.

Jones R. and Pendlebury M. (1996) *Public sector accounting*, 4th edition, London: Pitman Publishing.

Kähler J. and Sargeant A. (2002) 'The size effect in the administration cost of charities', *European Accounting Review*, 11: 215-243.

Kamath R. and Oberst E.R. (1992) 'Capital budgeting practices of large hospitals', *Engineering Economist*, 37: 203-232.

Kanter R.M. and Summers D.V. (1987) 'Doing well when doing good: Dilemma's of performance measurement in non-profit organisations and the need for a multiple-constituency approach', in Powell W.W. (ed.) *The non-profit sector: A research handbook*, New Haven: Yale University Press.

Kaplow L. (1995) 'A note on subsdising gifts', *Journal of Public Economics*, 58: 469-477.

Kapur K. and Weisbrod B.A. (2000) 'The roles of government and non-profit suppliers in mixed industries', *Public Finance Review*, 28: 275-308.

Karlan D. and List A. (2007) 'Does price matter in charitable giving? Evidence from a large-scale natural field experiment', *American Economic Review*, 97: 1774-1793.

Katz E. and Rosenberg J. (2005) 'An economic interpretation of institutional volunteering', *European Journal of Political Economy*, 21: 429-443.

Keating E.K., Fischer M., Gordon T.P. and Greenlee J. (2005) 'Assessing financial vulnerability in the non-profit sector', Harvard University, Working Paper RWP05-02.

Keating E.K., Parsons L.M. and Roberts A.A. (2008) 'Misreporting fundraising: how do non-profit organisations account for telemarketing campaigns?', *Accounting Review*, 83: 417-446.

Kessler D.P. and McClellan M.B. (2000) 'Is hospital competition socially wasteful?', *Quarterly Journal of Economics*, 115: 488-506.

— (2002) The effect of hospital ownership on medical productivity. *Rand Journal of Economics,* 33: 488-506.

Kingma B.R. (1997) 'Public good theories of the non-profit sector: Weisbrod revisited', *Voluntas: International Journal of Voluntary and Non-profit Organisations,* 8: 135-148.

Kitching K. (2009) 'Audit value and charitable organisations', *Journal of Accounting and Public Policy,* 28: 510-524.

Knox K.J., Blankmeyer E.C. and Stutzman J.R. (2006) 'Comparative performance and quality among non-profit nursing facilities in Texas', *Non-profit and Voluntary Sector Quarterly,* 35: 631-667.

Koning P. (2008) 'Not-for-profit provision of job training and mediation services: an empirical analysis using contract data of job training service providers' *Economist,* 156: 221-239.

Krashinsky M. (1986) 'Transaction costs and a theory of the non-profit organisation', in Rose-Ackerman S. (ed.) *The economics of non-profit organisations,* New York: J. Wiley.

Krishnan J. and Schauer P.C. (2000) 'The differentiation of quality among auditors: Evidence from the non-for-profit sector', *Auditing: A Journal of Practice and Theory,* 19: 9-25.

Krishnan R., Yetman M.H. and Yetman R.J (2004) 'Financial disclosure management by non-profit organisations', University of California at Davis, Working Paper.

— (2006) 'Expense misreporting in non-profit organisations', *Accounting Review,* 81: 399-420.

Lakdawalla D. and Philipson T. (2006) 'The non-profit sector and industry performance', *Journal of Public Economics,* 90: 1681-1698.

Landry C.E., Lange A., List J.A., Price M.K. and Rupp N.G. (2006) 'Toward an understanding of the economics of charity: Evidence from a field experiment', *Quarterly Journal of Economics,* 121: 747-782.

Lanfranchi J. and Narci M. (2008) 'Différence de satisfaction dans l'emploi entre secteurs à but lucratif et à but non lucratif: le rôle joué par les caractéristiques d'emploi' [Job satisfaction differentials between non-profit and for-profit sectors: the role of the job's characteristics], *Annals of Public and Cooperative Economics,* 79: 323-368.

Lange A. and Stocking A. (2009) 'Charitable memberships, volunteering, and discounts: evidence from a large-scale online field experiment', NBER Working Paper 14941, Washington DC: NBER.

Laughlin R.C. (1990) 'A model of financial accountability and the Church of England', *Financial Accountability and Management,* 6: 93–114.

Lavy V. (2008) 'Does rising the principal's wage improve school outcomes? Quasi-experimental evidence from an unusual policy experiment in Israel', *Scandinavian Journal of Economics,* 110: 639-662.

— (2010) 'Performance pay and teachers' effort, productivity, and grading ethics', *American Economic Review,* 99: 1979-2011.

Lee S.-Y.D., Alexander J.A., Wang V., Margolin F.S. and Combes J.R. (2008) 'An empirical taxonomy of hospital governing board roles', *Health Services Research,* 43: 1223-1243.

Leete L. (2001) 'Whither the non-profit wage differential? Estimates from the 1990 Census', *Journal of Labor Economics*, 19: 136-170.

Leone A.J. and Van Horn R.L. (2005) 'How do non-profit hospitals manage earnings?', *Journal of Health Economics,* 24: 815-837.

Lev B., Petrovits C. and Radhakrishnan S. (2010) 'Is doing good good for you? Howx corporate charitable contributions enhance revenue growth', *Strategic Management Journal*, 31: 182-200.

Lewis D. (2001) *The management of non-governmental development organisations: An introduction*, London: Routledge.

Liao-Troth M.A. and Dunn C.P. (1999) 'Social constructs and human service: Managerial sensemaking of volunteer motivation', *Voluntas: International Journal of Voluntary and Non-profit Organisations*, 10: 345-361.

Lichtenstein D.R., Drumwright M.E. and Braig B.M. (2004) 'The effect of Corporate Social Responsibility on customer donations to corporate supported non-profits', *Journal of Marketing*, 68: 16-32.

Ligon J.A. (1997) 'The capital structure of hospitals and reimbursement policy', *Quarterly Review of Economics and Finance*, 37: 59-77.

Lindrooth R.C. and Weisbrod B.A. (2007) 'Do religious non-profit and for-profit organisations respond differently to financial initiatives?', *Journal of Health Economics*, 26: 342-357.

Liu Y. and Weinberg C.B. (2004) 'Are non-profits unfair competitors for business? An analytic approach', *Journal of Public Policy and Marketing*, 23: 65-79.

Louviere J.J., Hensher D.A. and Swait J.D. (2000) *Stated choice methods: Analysis and application*, Cambridge: Cambridge University Press.

Lynk W.J. (1995) 'Non-profit hospital mergers and the exercise of market power', *Journal of Law and Economics*, 38: 437-461.

Lyons M. (1993) 'The history of non-profit organisations in Australia as a test of some recent non-profit theory', *Voluntas: International Journal of Voluntary and Non-profit Organisations*, 4: 301-325.

Maddison D. and Foster T. (2003) 'Valuing congestion costs in the British Museum', *Oxford Economic Papers*, 55: 173-190.

Maijoor S. (1991) *The economics of accounting regulation: Effects of Dutch accounting regulations for public accountants and firms,* Maastricht: Datawyse.

Malani A., Philipson T. and David G. (2003) 'Theories of firm behavior in the non-profit sector: A synthesis and empirical evaluation', in Glaeser E.L. (ed.) *The governance of not-for-profit firms*, Chicago: University of Chicago Press.

Marudas N.P. and Jacobs F.A. (2004) 'Determinants of charitable donations to large US higher education, hospital and scientific research non-profit organisations: New evidence from panel data', *Voluntas: International Journal of Voluntary and Non-profit Organisations*, 15: 157–179.

— (2010) 'Initial evidence on whether use of professional fundraising services increases fundraising effectiveness', *International Journal of Non-profit and Voluntary Sector Marketing*, 15: 3-12.

Marx J.D. (1999) 'Corporate philantropy: What is the strategy?', *Non-profit and Voluntary Sector Quarterly*, 28: 185-198.

Matsunaga Y. and Yamauchi N. (2004) 'Is the government failure theory still relevant? A panel analysis using US state level data', *Annals of Public and Cooperative Economics*, 75: 227-263.

Meier S. (2007) 'Do subsidies increase charitable giving in the long run? Matching donations in a field experiment', *Journal of the European Economic Association*, 6: 1203-1222.

Meijer M.-M., De Bakker F.G., Smit J.H. and Schuyt T. (2006) 'Corporate giving in the Netherlands 1995-2003: Exploring the amounts involved and the motivations for donating', *International Journal of Non-profit and Voluntary Sector Marketing*, 11: 13-28.

Menchik P.L. and Weisbrod B.A. (1987) 'Volunteer labor supply', *Journal of Public Economics,* 32: 159-183.

Middleton M. (1987) 'Non-profit boards of directors beyond the governance function', in Powell W.W. (ed.) *The non-profit sector: A research handbook,* New Haven: Yale University Press.

Middleton M. and Greer C. (1996) 'Planning in ambiguous contexts: The dilemma of meeting needs for commitment and demands for legitimacy', *Strategic Management Journal*, 17: 633-652.

Milgrom, P. and Roberts, J. (1992) *Economics, organisation and management,* Englewood Cliffs: Prentice-Hall.

Miller J.L. (2002) 'The board as a monitor of organisational activity: The applicability of agency theory to non-profit boards', *Non-profit Management and Leadership*, 12: 429-450.

Miller K.D. (2002) 'Competitive strategies of religious organisations', *Strategic Management Journal*, 23: 435-456.

Miller-Millesen J.L. (2003) 'Understanding the behavior of non-profit boards of directors: A theory based approach', *Non-profit and Voluntary Sector Quarterly*, 32: 521-547.

Minkoff D.C. and Powell W.W. (2006) 'Non-profit mission: Constancy, responsiveness, or deflection?', in Powell W.W. and Steinberg R. (eds.) *The non-profit sector: A research handbook*, 2nd edition, New Haven: Yale University Press.

Mobley L.R. and Bradford W.D. (1997) 'Behavioural differences among hospitals: Is it ownership, or location?', *Applied Economics*, 29: 1125-1138.

Mocan H.N. and Tekin E. (2003) 'Non-profit sector and part-time work: An analysis of employer-employee matched data on child care workers', *Review of Economics and Statistics*, 85: 38-50.

Mook L., Handy F. and Quarter J. (2007) 'Reporting volunteer labor at the organisational level: A study of Canadian non-profits', *Voluntas: International Journal of Voluntary and Non-profit Organisations*, 18: 55-71.

Moore M.H. (2000) 'Managing for value: Organisational strategy in for-profit, non-profit, and governmental organisations', *Non-profit and Voluntary Sector Quarterly*, 29 (Supplement): 183-204.

Morris, S. (2000) 'Defining the non-profit sector: Some lessons from history', *Voluntas: International Journal of Voluntary and Non-profit Organisations*, 11: 25-43.

Mosca M., Musella M. and Pastore F. (2007) 'Relational goods, monitoring and non-pecuniary compensations in the non-profit sector: The case of the Italian social services', *Annals of Public and Cooperative Economics*, 78: 57-86.

Prüfer J. (2010) 'Competition and mergers among nonprofits', *Joural of Competition Law and Economics*, 7: 69-92.

Prieto-Rodríguez J. and Fernández-Blanco V. (2006) 'Optimal pricing an grant policies for museums', *Journal of Cultural Economics*, 30: 169-181.

Rayburn J.M. and Rayburn L.G. (1991) 'Contingency theory and the impact of new accounting technology in uncertain hospital environments', *Accounting, Auditing and Accountability Journal*, 4: 55-75.

Reed P.B. and Selbee L.K. (2000) 'Distinguishing characteristics of active volunteers in Canada', *Non-profit and Voluntary Sector Quarterly*, 29: 571-592.

Ritchie W.J. and Eastwood K. (2006) 'Executive functional experience and its relationship to the financial performance of non-profit organisations', *Non-profit Management and Leadership*, 17: 67-82.

Robbins K.C. (2006) 'The non-profit sector in historical perspective: Traditions of philanthropy in the West', in Powell W.W. and Steinberg R. (eds.) *The non-profit sector: A research handbook*, 2nd edition, New Haven: Yale University Press.

Robbins W.A., Turpin R. and Polinski P. (1993) 'Economic incentives and accounting choice strategy by non-profit hospitals', *Financial Accountability and Management*, 9: 159–175.

Rogelberg S.G., Allen J.A., Conway J.M., Goh A., Currie L. and McFarland B. (2010) 'Employee experiences with volunteers: assessment, description, antecedents, and outcomes', *Non-profit Management and Leadership*, 20: 423-444.

Roomkin M.J. and Weisbrod B.A. (1999) 'Managerial compensation and incentives in for-profit and non-profit hospitals', *Journal of Law, Economics and Organisation*, 15: 750-781.

Rose-Ackerman S. (1987) 'Ideals versus dollars: Donor, charity managers, and government grants', *Journal of Political Economy*, 95: 810-823.

— (1996) 'Altruism, non-profits, and economic theory', *Journal of Economic Literature*, 34: 701-728.

Ruhm C.J. and Borkoski C. (2004) 'Compensation in the non-profit sector', *Journal of Human Resources*, 38: 992-1021.

Salamon G.L. (1985) 'Accounting rates of return', *American Economic Review*, 75: 495-504.

Salamon, L.M. (1987) 'Partners in public service: The scope and theory of government-non-profit relations', in Powell W.W. (ed.) *The non-profit sector: A research handbook*, New Haven: Yale University Press.

Salamon, L.M. and Anheier H.K. (1992a) 'In search of the non-profit sector I: The question of definitions', *Voluntas: International Journal of Voluntary and Non-profit Organisations*, 3: 125-151.

— (1992b) 'In search of the non-profit sector II: The problem of classification', *Voluntas: International Journal of Voluntary and Non-profit Organisations*, 3: 267-309.

— (1998) 'Social origins of civil society: Explaining the non-profit sector cross-nationally', *Voluntas: International Journal of Voluntary and Non-profit Organisations*, 9: 213-248.

Sampson S.E. (2006) 'Optimisation of volunteer labor assignments', *Journal of Operations Management*, 24:363-377.

Sansing R. (1998) 'The Unrelated Business Income Tax, cost allocation, and productive efficiency', *National Tax Journal*, 51: 281-302.

Sargeant A. (2005) *Marketing management for non-profit organisations*, 2nd edition, Oxford: Oxford University Press.

Sargeant A. and Woodliffe L. (2008) 'Individual giving behaviour: a multidisciplinary review', in Sargeant, A. and Wymer, W. (eds) *The Routledge companion to non-profit marketing*, London: Routledge.

Sargeant A. and Wymer W. (eds) (2008) *The Routledge companion to non-profit marketing*, London: Routledge.

Sargeant A., Wymer W. and Hilton T. (2006) 'Marketing bequest club membership: An exploratory study of legacy pledgers', *Non-profit and Voluntary Sector Quarterly*, 35: 384-404.

Schepers C., De Gieter S., Pepermans R., Du Bois C., Caers R. and Jegers M. (2005) 'How are employees of the non-profit sector motivated? A research need', *Non-profit Management and Leadership*, 16: 191-208.

Schiff J. and Weisbrod B. (1991) 'Competition between for-profit and non-profit organisations in commercial markets', *Annals of Public and Cooperative Economics* 62: 619-639.

Schlesinger M., Mitchell S. and Gray B.H. (2004) 'Restoring public legitimacy to the non-profit sector: A survey experiment using descriptions of non-profit ownership', *Non-profit and Voluntary Sector Quarterly*, 33: 673-710.

Shapiro B.P. (1973) 'Marketing for non-profit organisations', *Harvard Business Review*, 5: 123-132, in Gies D.L., Ott, J.S. and Shafritz J.M. (eds.) (1990) *The non-profit organisation. Essential readings*, Pacific Grove: Brooks/Cole.

Shoham A., Ruvio A., Vigoda-Gadot E. and Schwabsky N. (2006) 'Market orientation in the non-profit and voluntary sector: A meta-analysis of their relationships with organisational performance', *Non-profit and Voluntary Sector Quarterly*, 35: 453-476.

Silvergleid J.E. (2003) 'Effects of watchdog organisations on the social capital market', *New Directions for Philanthropic Fundraising*, 41: 7-26.

Sinitsyn M. and Weisbrod B.A. (2008) 'Behavior of non-profit organisations in for-profit markets: the curious case of unprofitable revenue-raising activities', *Journal of Institutional and Theoretical Economics*, 164: 727-750.

Skinner M.W. and Rosenberg M.W. (2006) 'Managing competition in the countryside: Non-profit and for-profit perceptions of long-term care in rural Ontario', *Social Science and Medicine*, 63: 2864-2876.

Sloan F.A. (1988) 'Property rights in the hospital industry', in Frech H.E. (ed.) *Health care in America: The political economy of hospitals and health insurance*, San Francisco: PRIPP.

Sloan F.A, Valvona J., Hassan M. and Morrisey M.A. (1988) 'Cost of capital to the hospital sector', *Journal of Health Economics*, 7: 25-45.

Sloan M.F. (2009) 'The effects of non-profit accountability ratings on donor behavior', *Non-profit and Voluntary Sector Quarterly*, 38: 220-236.

Smith D.H. and Shen C. (1996) 'Factors characterising the most effective non-profits managed by volunteers', *Non-profit Leadership and Management*, 6: 271-289.

Smith T.M. (2007) 'The impact of government funding on private contributions to non-profit performing arts organisations', *Annals of Public and Cooperative Economics*, 78: 137-160.

Song S. and Yi D.T. (2011) 'The fundraising efficiency in US non-profit art organizations: an application of a Bayesian estimation approach using the stochastic frontier production model', *Journal of Productivity Analysis*, 35: 171-180.

Steinberg R. (1986a) 'Should donors care about fundraising?', in Rose-Ackerman S. (ed.) *The economics of non-profit organisations*, New York: J. Wiley.

— (1986b) 'The revealed objective functions of non-profit firms', *Rand Journal of Economics*, 17: 508-526.

— (1987) 'Non-profit organisations and the market', in Powell W.W. (ed.) *The non-profit sector: A research handbook*, New Haven: Yale University Press.

— (1990) 'Profits and incentive compensation in non-profit firms', *Non-profit Management and Leadership*, 1: 137-152.

— (1993) 'Public policy and the performance of non-profit organisations: A general framework', *Non-profit and Voluntary Sector Quarterly*, 22: 13–31.

— (2004) 'Introduction', in Steinberg R. (ed.) *The economics of non-profit enterprises*, Cheltenham: Edward Elgar.

— (2006) 'Economic theories of non-profit organisations', in Powell W.W. and Steinberg R. (eds.) *The non-profit sector: A research handbook*, 2nd edition, New Haven: Yale University Press.

Steinberg R. and Gray B.H. (1993) ' "The role of non-profit enterprise" in 1993: Hansmann revisited', *Non-profit and Voluntary Sector Quarterly*, 22: 297-316.

Stephens R.D., Dawley D.D. and Stephens D.B. (2004) 'Commitment on the board: a model of volunteer directors' levels of organisational commitment and self-reported performance', *Journal of Management Issues*, 16: 483-504.

Stone M.M., Bigelow B. and Crittenden W. (1999) 'Research on strategic management in non-profit organisations: Synthesis, analysis, and future directions', *Administration and Society*, 31: 378-423.

Sundeen R.A., Raskoff S.A. and Garcia M.C. (2007) 'Differences in perceived barriers to volunteering to formal organisations: Lack of time versus lack of interest', *Non-profit Management and Leadership*, 17: 279-300.

Tao H.-L. and Yeh P. (2007) 'Religion as an investment: Comparing the contributions and volunteer frequency among Christians, Buddhists, and folk religionists', *Southern Economic Journal*, 73: 770-790.

Tate S.L. (2007) 'Auditor change and auditor choice in non-profit organisations', *Auditing: A Journal of Practice and Theory*, 26: 47-70.

Thornton J. (2006) 'Non-profit fund-raising in competitive donor markets', *Non-profit and Voluntary Sector Quarterly*, 35: 204-224.

— (2010) 'Explaining unrestricted giving by charitable foundations: a transaction cost approach', *International Journal of Industrial Organisation*, 28: 44-53.

Thornton J.P. and Belski W.H. (2010) 'Financial reporting quality and price competition among non-profit firms', *Applied Economics*, 42: 2699-2713.

Thornton J. and Cave L. (2010) 'The effects of organisational form in the mixed market for foster care', *Annals of Public and Cooperative Economics*, 81: 211-245.

Tinkelman D. (1998) 'Differences in sensitivity of financial statement users to joint allocations: The case of non-profit organisations', *Journal of Accounting, Auditing and Finance*, 13: 377-393.

— (2004) 'Using non-profit organisation-level financial data to infer managers' fund-raising strategies', *Journal of Public Economics*, 88: 2181-2191.

— (2006) 'The decision-usefulness of non-profit fundraising ratios: Some contrary evidence', *Journal of Accounting, Auditing and Finance*, 21: 441-462.

— (2009) 'Unintended consequences of expense ratio guidelines: the Avon breast cancer walks', *Journal of Accounting and Public Policy*, 28: 485-494.

— (2010) 'Revenue interactions: crowding out, crowding in, or neither?', in Seaman, B.A. and Young, D.R. (eds) *Handbook of research on non-profit economics and management*, Cheltenham: Edward Elgar.

Tinkelman D. and Mankaney K. (2007) 'When is administrative efficiency associated with charitable donations?', *Non-profit and Voluntary Sector Quarterly*, 36: 41-64.

Trigg R. and Nabangi F.K. (1995) 'Representation of the financial position of non-profit organisations: The Habitat for Humanity situation', *Financial Accountability and Management*, 11: 259-269.

Trussel J.M. (2002) 'Revisiting the prediction of financial vulnerability', *Non-profit Management and Leadership*, 13: 17-31.

— (2003) 'Assessing potential accounting manipulation: The financial characteristics of charitable organisations with higher than expected program-spending ratios', *Non-profit and Voluntary Sector Quarterly*, 32: 616-634.

Tuckman H.P. (1993) 'How and why non-profit organisations obtain capital', in Hammack D.C. and Young D.R. (eds.) *Non-profit organisations in a market economy*, San Francisco: Jossey-Bass.

— (1998a) 'Competition, commercialisation, and the evolution of non-profit organisational structures', *Journal of Policy Analysis and Management*, 17: 175-194.

— (1998b) 'Competition, commercialisation, and the evolution of non-profit organisational structures', in Weisbrod B.A. (ed.) *To profit or not to profit: The commercial transformation of the non-profit sector*, Cambridge: Cambridge University Press.

— (2009) 'The strategic and economic value of hybrid non-profit structures', in Cordes, J.J. and Steuerle, C.E. (eds) *Non-profits & business*, Washington DC: The Urban Institute Press.

Tuckman H.P. and Chang C.F. (1988) 'Cost convergence between for-profit and non-for-profit nursing homes: Does competition matter?' *Quarterly Review of Economics and Business*, 28: 50-65.

United Nations (2003) *Handbook on non-profit institutions in the system of national accounts*. New York: United Nations.

Valentinov V. (2006) 'Non-profit organisation and the division of labor: A theoretical perspective', *Atlantic Economic Journal*, 34: 435-447.

— (2007) 'Some reflections on the transaction cost theory of non-profit organisations', *Zeitschrift für öffentliche und gemeinwirtschaftliche Unternehmen (Journal for Public and Non-profit Services)*, 30: 52-67.

— (2008a) 'The economics of non-profit organisation: in search of an integrative theory', *Journal of Economic Issues*, 42: 745-761.

— (2008b) 'The economics of the non-distribution constraint: a critical reappraisal', *Annals of Public and Cooperative Economics*, 79: 35-52.

Van Diepen M., Donkers B. and Franses P.H. (2009) 'Dynamic and competitive effects of direct mailings: a charitable giving application', *Journal of Marketing Research*, 46: 120-133.

Vermeer T.E., Raghunandan K. and Forgione D.A. (2006) 'The composition of non-profit audit committees', *Accounting Horizons*, 20: 75-90.

— (2009) 'Audit fees at U.S. non-profit organisations', *Auditing: a Journal of Practice and Theory*, 28: 289-303.

Verschueren I. and Jegers M. (2004) 'The capital structure of cultural non-profit organisations: Theory and US evidence', paper presented at the European Institute for Advanced Studies in Management Workshop Managing Cultural Organisations, Bologna.

Vita M.G. and Sacher S. (2001) 'The competitive effects of not-for-profit hospital mergers: A case study', *Journal of Industrial Economics*, 49: 63-84.

Vitaliano D.F. (2003) 'Do not-for-profit firms maximise profits?', *Quarterly Review of Economics and Finance*, 43: 75-87.

Watts R.L. and Zimmerman J.L. (1986) *Positive accounting theory*, Englewood Cliffs: Prentice Hall.

— (1990) 'Positive accounting theory: A ten year perspective', *Accounting Review*, 65: 131-156.

Wedig G.J. (1994) 'Risk, leverage, donations and dividends-in-kind: A theory of non-profit financial behavior', *International Review of Economics and Finance*, 3: 257-278.

Wedig G.J., Hassan M. and Morrisey M.A. (1996) 'Tax-exempt debt and the capital structure of non-profit organisations: An application to hospitals', *Journal of Finance*, 51: 1247-1283.

Wedig G.J. and Kwon S. (1995) 'Sustainable asset growth and the accounting rate of return in not-for-profit organisations: Theory and evidence', *International Journal of Economics and Business*, 2: 367-391.

Wedig G.J., Sloan F.A., Hassan M. and Morrisey M.A. (1988) 'Capital structure, ownership, and capital payment policy: The case of hospitals', *Journal of Finance*, 43: 21-40.

Weisbrod, B.A. (1988) *The non-profit economy*, Cambridge: Harvard University Press.

— (1998) 'The non-profit mission and its financing: Growing links between non-profits and the rest of the economy', in Weisbrod B.A. (ed.) *To profit or not to profit: The commercial transformation of the non-profit sector*, Cambridge: Cambridge University Press.

Werker E. and Ahmed F.Z. (2008) 'What do nongovernmental organisations do?', *Journal of Economic Perspectives*, 22: 73-92.

Williamson O.E. (1979) 'Transaction-cost economics: The governance of contractual relations', *Journal of Law and Economics*, 22: 233-261.

— (1983) 'Organisational form, residual claimants, and corporate control', *Journal of Law and Economics*, 26: 351-366.

— (1991) 'Comparative economic organisation: The analysis of discrete structural alternatives', *Adminstrative Science Quarterly*, 36: 269-296.

Yan W., Denison D.V. and Butler J.S. (2009) 'Revenue structure and non-profit borrowing', *Public Finance Review*, 37: 47-67.

Yetman M.H. and Yetman R.J. (2003) 'The effect of non-profits' taxable activities on the supply of private donations', *National Tax Journal*, 56: 243-258.

— (2004) 'The effects of governance on the financial reporting quality of non-profit organisations', paper presented at the Conference on not-for-profit firms, Federal Reserve Bank, New York.

Yetman, M.H., Yetman, R.J. and Badertscher B. (2009) 'Calibrating the reliability of publicly available non-profit taxable activity disclosures: comparing IRS900 and IRS900-T data', *Non-profit and Voluntary Sector Quarterly*, 38: 95-116.

Yetman R.J (2001) 'Tax-motivated expense allocations by non-profit organisations', *Accounting Review*, 76: 297-311.

Yörük B.K. (2008) 'The power of asking in volunteering: evidence from a matched sample', *Economics Letters*, 99: 79-84.

Young D.R. (1987) 'Executive leadership in non-profit organisations', in Powell W.W. (ed.) *The non-profit sector: A research handbook*, New Haven: Yale University Press.

— (2000) 'Alternative models of government-non-profit sector relations: Theoretical and international perspectives', *Non-profit and Voluntary Sector Quarterly*, 29: 149-172.

— (2009) 'Alternative perspectives on social enterprise', in Cordes, J.J. and Steuerle, C.E. (eds) *Non-profits & business*, Washington DC: The Urban Institute Press.

— (2010) 'Franchises and federations: the economics of multi-site non-profit organisations', in Seaman, B.A. and Young, D.R. (eds) *Handbook of research on non-profit economics and management*, Cheltenham: Edward Elgar.

Young D.R. and Steinberg R. (1995) *Economics for non-profit managers*, New York: The Foundation Center.

Zaleski P.A. and Esposito A.G. (2007) 'The response to market power: Non-profit hospitals versus for-profit hospitals', *Atlantic Economic Journal*, 35: 315-325.